Little Seed Publishing
Laguna Beach, CA

COPYRIGHT © 2009, by Global Partnership, LLC

Pre-press Management by New Caledonian Press
Text Design: Angie Kimbro

Cover Design and Illustrations: K-Squared Designs, LLC, www.k2ds.com

Publisher intends this material for entertainment and no legal, medical or other professional advice is implied or expressed. If the purchaser cannot abide by this statement, please return the book for a full refund.

Acknowledgement is made for permission to quote copyrighted materials.

Publisher acknowledges that certain chapters were originally published in similar or identical form in other *Wake Up...Live the Life You Love* books and reprinted by permission of Little Seed Publishing, with all rights reserved.

For information, contact Little Seed Publishing's operations office at Global Partnership: P.O. Box 894, Murray, KY 42071, or phone 270-753-5225 (CST).

Distributed by Global Partnership, LLC
P.O. Box 894
Murray, KY 42071

Library of Congress Cataloguing in Publication Data
Wake Up... Live the Life You Love: In Service
ISBN-13: 978-1-933063-17-1

$14.95 USA $14.95 Canada   £9.95 UK

Other books by Steven E, and Lee Beard

Wake Up...Live the Life You Love:
...First Edition
...Second Edition
...Inspirational How-to Stories
...In Beauty
...Living on Purpose
...Finding Your Life's Passion
...Purpose, Passion, Abundance
...Finding Personal Freedom
...Seizing Your Success
...Giving Gratitude
...On the Enlightened Path
...In Spirit
...Finding Life's Passion
...Stories of Transformation
...A Search for Purpose
...Living In Abundance
...The Power of Team
...Living In Clarity
...Wake Up Moments
...Wake Up Moments of Inspiration
...Empowered

Wake Up...Shape Up...Live the Life You Love

WAKE UP...
LIVE THE LIFE YOU LOVE

In Service

TABLE OF CONTENTS

INTRODUCTION

Unfortunately, service is something many of us seek to avoid. We operate under the assumption that being in service to others means we will have to give too much of ourselves—we will lose who we are in the process. We feel we won't be able to be what we desire; we will be stuck serving the whims of others. We fear that we will lose ourselves if we are not at the center of all. The good news is, this is not what it means to be in service!

The answer to this dilemma, as Steven E says, is to first "find your purpose." Purpose is what gives us the drive to work hard doing what we love. "When people ask me, 'How can I serve,'" Steven E observes, "I tell them to first discover their purpose in life. Then, you will see how you can serve others while at the same time enriching your own life." In other words, real satisfaction and benefit comes from being a giver.

In order to find your purpose and to discover how you can best serve others while empowering yourself, there are some key questions you need to ask. First, what is it you enjoy doing most? Next, how can you turn your passion into something you do regularly? Once you have solved these issues, find a way to be in service. Ask yourself what others have done that was of service to you. Study their lives and practices. Make them examples and branch out in your own unique, creative way.

In this book you will find help in answering these questions. You will meet dynamic individuals who learned from experience to first discover what they were made to do and who then focused their passion outwards toward others. This is not merely a "how-to" book, but a powerful encounter with several individuals who have learned the answers to those tough questions, taken charge and are now living in service. These are their stories—your story has yet to be written.

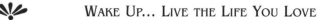

WAKE UP...
LIVE THE LIFE YOU LOVE

In Service

A LIFE OF JOYFUL SERVICE
Steven E

Putting yourself in the position to serve others is something that, surprisingly, will benefit you in the long run. First and foremost, serving others ultimately comes from the heart. It's not a lifestyle you can intellectually attain. The energy you put out into the world comes back to you in a way beyond human understanding. The mystery I'm speaking of is profound, yet quite simple; the more you engage in serving others, the more you are able to find personal fulfillment.

When I had my wake up moment, one of the things I realized was that I had been living for myself. I awoke in the night with the revelation that I should write a book that would help others. It was as if I had discovered my purpose, then and there. My dream soon became a reality and eventually evolved into the *Wake Up Live* book series through which I have been able to help countless people find their own paths to peace, love and service to others. These blessings have returned to me a hundredfold. Nothing brings greater joy to my life than helping others find ways to serve, and in turn, find peace in themselves.

There is a constant temptation to become negative and selfish, to think that we will find fulfillment if we focus completely on our own immediate monetary or emotional needs. This, again, denies the basic principle outlined before, that the good energies you put into the world will come back to you. The sooner you recognize this, the sooner you will find that good things "come back around."

In all of our relationships, we must first go within and be at peace with ourselves, giving our hearts and minds the service they deserve. From there we move outward toward others, conveying the same peace that we found within ourselves. For example, if you have moved inward and treated yourself to kindness and unconditional love, you will then be able to project those same caring emotions to those who are intimate friends, and even to those you don't yet know beyond mere acquaintance.

We all crave personal, spiritual growth. However, another temptation we often encounter is the mistaken idea that we gain personal growth through physical means such as attaining more money or material assets. The fact of the matter is we were made for something more. We were made for creating loving relationships with others through service. Being in service to others is truly the gateway to happiness and fulfillment after having found it within. That is exactly how I found it!

Steven E

CUSTOMER SERVICE IS COMMON SENSE
Jeffrey Lestz and Bob Safford, Jr.

There are exceptional individuals who rekindle our hope that we are someone special. The feeling we have when we are exposed to such people is among the most pleasant, reassuring and infectious we can have. After just one experience, we find ourselves wanting to be like them—to help others and spread the wonderful feeling which was shared with us.

These people are not necessarily the Mother Teresa's of the world. They are not teachers, missionaries or wealthy benefactors of generous foundations. They are the people right in front of us when we need something; they are business owners, managers, customer service people and government clerks. Their mission is to get us what we need, deserve and pay for. Sadly, most of us can remember more times of disappointment than pleasure when we reflect on our everyday experiences. Let us start with some good news. Here is Bob's story:

Recently, I purchased a rather large gas grill from a department store. I was not impressed with the ability or attentiveness of the salesperson as my son and I made our selection, but the young man who helped us load the multiple boxes was a delight. He even offered suggestions about how the three of us might solve the puzzle of getting 30 cubic feet of boxes into 28 cubic feet of car! After arriving home and assembling the monster grill, we discovered that the very last piece had been badly bent in shipping.

I returned to the store the next day with receipt in hand, loins girded and sword drawn expecting a battle. It never came. The young man in the garden department could not have possibly been more helpful or friendly. He didn't even look at the receipt. He took down my details, called the factory for me, completed all the paperwork on my behalf and sent me on my way with a handshake. He smiled and promised to call when it came in. One week later he called as promised. Because we love it when we are treated with extra care, I now have become a loyal customer of this department store.

Unfortunately, this is no longer the norm. Take the example of customer service in the airline industry. Forget fees for luggage, checking yourself in online, and two dollars for a soft drink. Recently, for a family trip, Bob's family took a cruise, but first needed to fly to Florida from Philadelphia. The airline lost three of eight bags. Forget the details about why the baggage handlers never put them on the plane, or the next two planes, the four-hour wait at the Fort Lauderdale airport with his brother-in-law or dealing with "customer service." The bags never made it to the ship.

Bob's wife, daughter and son had to vacation without luggage. They maintained a great attitude and had fun anyway. The cruise line was very helpful and had a terrific system for taking care of passengers in this predicament. The airline, on the other hand, did only what was required. Eventually, they found the bags and got them to the last port before the return home. They never apologized, but supplied the form so Bob could make the claim to their third party insurance company.

Bob came away feeling frustrated and used. He had expected better treatment—especially as a card-carrying deluxe, platinum, super-duper frequent flyer. Where was the customer service? Where was the "extra mile?" We all would prefer to be treated well rather than being given a bunch of "mileage points" that are as difficult to redeem as a Las Vegas poker chip at the Bank of England. Can I trade 5,000 miles to get a little respect?

In today's very competitive business world company profits are driven by short-term quarterly reports. As business people, we can understand the dilemma. These days share prices are influenced, to a large degree, by institutional investors. Money managers are looking at the bottom line. If there is one poor quarter to forgive, the next poor quarter finds the CEO under pressure to either cut or be cut. This leaves the customer holding the short end of the stick.

People deserve more. That is why, when we started Genistar, Ltd., in the United Kingdom, we determined that we would set a new standard of excellence for customer service in the UK—and not just among financial services companies, but all companies! Our goal was to have people say to apathetic airlines, curt customer service agents and temperamental telephone companies, "Why can't you be more like Genistar?"

We founded Genistar on dual maxims, "Always do what is right for the consumer," and "Always tell the truth." We know these are old fashioned principles of honesty and giving, but should not be unusual. Yet, often in these fast-paced times, it seems to be all about automated service. By the time you get to a real person (if ever you do) you either forgot why you called or are so frustrated with pushing buttons, giving passwords and codes that you feel you need a handful of aspirin. What ever happened to, "The customer is king?" or "Service with a smile?" In fact, what happened to service?

Call us old fashioned, but we believe in integrity, honesty and good service. We are not perfect, but our hope and intentions are to be the best service company in the nation and do everything we can to give the consumer a helping hand. We believe if you take care of the customer and your associates like family, they will stay with you—why should they go elsewhere? We show families how to save money by budgeting and finding solid financial directions. We call it giving them a P.H.D.— Proper Honest Direction. You cannot do that with an answering machine.

In this book are the stories of many other successful people and companies who are leading by example; those who have made the hard choice to be different, lead in their community or industry and set a new standard of excellence in service to others. Since you are reading this book, maybe you are also preparing to lead your firm or industry to a new level of service. We hope that you join all of us in following a 2,000-year-old teaching and go with us the "extra mile."

No one has ever complained when he or she received more than what he or she paid for. Perhaps—just perhaps—the attitude will be passed along through friendliness and charity in the person's family and business life. Service is the gift that keeps on giving.

Jeffrey Lestz and Bob Safford, Jr.

SERVICE: LIFE'S CURRENCY
Shabana Ahmad

Have you ever wondered how you ended up living the life you are living? Is it truly a life you love, or is it a life you have comfortably accepted?

Although many people can't or won't answer that question on its face, I think we all know the answer if we simply look within. More than 12 years ago, I made a choice that put me on the path that led to my "wake up." That choice was the defining moment in my life.

My choice was to have a child out of wedlock. For many people, that may not seem monumental. Women do it every day, right? Well, it was monumental for me because of my heritage and, specifically, my cultural and religious upbringing.

For me, the hardest part about that decision was understanding the change within my family, with some of my friends and, at times, within me. After I made my choice, they spoke of my potential as something I had lost forever. My decision not only redefined me, but it now defined my opportunities—or the lack of opportunities—in the future. I was no longer seen as someone with limitless potential, but as a single mom. My choice had surely sealed my fate. I would become a statistic. A lifetime of welfare and poverty was all for which I could possibly hope. I was stunned and stupefied, but ultimately, I was just confused. Had the circumstances of my choice suddenly changed the possibilities for my life?

It's ironic because I suspect that my son was sent to teach me more than I think I could ever teach him. So far, he's taught me what real strength is, what courage really means and why selflessness is a greater friend than selfishness can ever be. He's also taught me that it is in our moments of decision that our destiny is made.

As the days, months and years have passed, I have watched him grow, stretch and take the risks that have been necessary for him to become who he is destined to be. In watching him, I have learned the importance of continuously growing. As adults, we become more and more unwilling to take risks. We want all the glory, but are unwilling to pay the price to reach our goals.

When I turned 30, I met a pivotal character in my life. His name is John Kanary. I mention him because he did for me what I now aspire to do for others. He asked the tough questions and challenged my thinking. Most importantly, he helped me recognize how the beliefs I held were, in fact, the only obstacles that kept getting in my way.

He suggested I take an inventory of my life, so I asked myself the very question I posed earlier. Are you living a life you truly love? The answer was not a resounding "yes", but it did whisper to me. I realized my life never became limited; it was only my thinking and the thoughts of others that forced me to limit myself. After all, I have done a great job raising an incredibly smart, understanding and compassionate child. I put myself through university and never spent a single day in poverty (although some of my tax returns would certainly suggest otherwise).

After completing the inventory, I made another choice. I decided I was only going to take advice from people who were getting the results I wanted to get. I would no longer heed the advice of people who were not getting those kinds of results. I sought those people who mirrored my faith in the human spirit. I looked for people who you know, just by looking at them, are successful in all areas of their lives. They have achieved the balance we all seek and they know something the masses don't. You could tell by the relationships they have with others and the kindness of their demeanor that they love their lives. The successes they enjoy are simply the by-products of whatever they know and I wanted to know what that was! I found conversations with those people always left me with a feeling of hope, empowerment and purpose. Most importantly, they always asked me what they could do to help me. How could they be of service to me? They never asked what was in it for them. They simply wanted me to know that if they could help, I should feel free to call them. I had unwittingly stumbled upon one of the keys to true success. To be in service to others is to add value and to be valuable. True success is not about what we get, it's about what we give—our contribution to the flow. That's the currency of life. I realized I found the key, and since then, the sky has been the limit!

It's the feeling you get when you help others get what they want; it's a selfish selflessness that transcends language, circumstances and our differences. I believe that every one of us is capable of great things. Most of us just don't know how to do it yet.

Today, I wake up with enthusiasm and actually resent the sleep that takes me away from the life I love so much. John had described that as a signal. At the time I didn't get it, but now that I understand, I have it forever. Now, the time I spend with people is spent with a servant's heart. I see limitless potential in every person I meet because I know it's there and because I know it's never too late to unleash it and become what you might have been. All one needs to do is decide, but the first step is the hardest.

The moment I decided my life was not about what I get, but what I give, I realized my life is, in fact, a journey. The purpose is not to race toward death. I began to live a life I love in service to others because, you see, we only get out what we put in and we only get to do life once. We have to bring our value to the table and play our A-game every day.

Those limiting beliefs of lack and scarcity cause many extraordinary people to settle for ordinary lives. They rob so many of the glorious feeling that comes when you resent the sleep that takes you away from your life. Since John Kanary was my bridge, in the spirit of service, my intention is to be that bridge for others to help fill the gap between the life they live and the life they would love to live. Ask yourself the question, take an inventory and move toward living a life you love. If you find you need some help, step out and seek the life that is and has always been seeking you.

Destiny is what you are meant to do. Fate is what happens when you aren't doing it.

Shabana Ahmad

A LIFESTYLE OF SERVICE
Robert Vance

S ervice is not something we do; it is a lifestyle we live.

Sir Winston Churchill said: "*We make a living by what we get, but we make a life by what we give.*" Most people live an ordinary life, but there are some who live an astonishing one. These are the people who, in addition to being highly successful in life, make a great contribution to society—the people who leave a legacy for future generations.

Serving is not necessarily about giving money to those in need. It is about giving of your time, talents or finances unconditionally and without expectation of return or reward. The person living the astonishing life is always looking for ways to make the world a better place. While there are some people who value their lives above all else, there are also those who value other lives above their own, but giving not only includes giving to others, but also to yourself. If you do not take care of yourself, you may come to the point where you feel like you cannot give any more and you get burnt out. Remember to also do things for yourself so you can continue to be of service to others. You must balance both.

Some people think they must look out for themselves because no one else will. They live in a world where there are winners and losers. Then there are those who choose a different path, and instead of seeing winners and losers, they see a world in which *they* win by helping *others* win.

The average person gives with the expectation of getting something back. They will not give unless there is something for them to gain. Then, there are the astonishing people who give without regard for what they will get back; they give because they are committed to making the world a better place.

I once had the most wonderful experience. I went with a group of people to the downtown area of a city in California. We were given the opportunity to find a local homeless shelter and were left there with no money, ID or possessions. The only thing we had was a bag lunch. During this time, I met some of the poor and sat down to share my lunch with two marvelous older ladies sitting on the sidewalk. As I sat there, I watched people walk by and completely ignore us. As I sat there talking, I discovered these two were people just like you and me, but had had a series of misfortunes that led to homelessness. The most touching moment occurred when I met back up with my group and the ladies directed me to take the train because the meeting place was quite a distance away. Then they gave me the two dollars for the train fare so I would not get in trouble for riding without a ticket. It touched me greatly because these ladies who had so little were willing to give what they had to help someone they perceived to be in need.

There are some people in this world who believe they cannot give because they do not have enough time, money, etc. to go around. This comes from a scarcity way of thinking. I prefer to believe there is an abundance of resources to tap into for helping others.

This reminds me of another experience I had while working with a charity that provides homes for people. Instead of simply giving people the house, the beneficiaries are required to contribute their time to help build their own house. Our project that day was to help build a house for each of two homeless families. They were currently living in a house consisting of a few boards put together, and they slept on a dirt floor.

When we showed up, the families were so excited. They pitched in to help hold a board here or get nails there. They were truly excited to receive this help. They did not have any of the skills required to build the house, but they did have the desire to help with anything they could.

Most people donate what they have an abundance of, which goes back to giving what one thinks is needed and not what is wanted. Astonishing people donate what they have less of. If you truly want to grow in life, give what you have little of. By doing this you will increase your capacity in this area. Average people hoard their skills out of a scarcity mentality. They are afraid that if other people have their knowledge, they might lose their own jobs. How much more valuable would you be to your company if you shared your knowledge with your co-workers?

Some successful people tend to give money instead of their time because they have more of that to give. They use financial giving as an excuse for not donating their time. This happens in many areas of life, including at home. They may give their spouses money to go get something to make up for missed dates. They may give their children toys to make up for missing soccer games. How much more fulfilled would their lives be if they took the time to give of themselves and spent time with their families instead of giving what they have an abundance of? What do you think the spouse or child would prefer? Have you thought to ask someone what he needs from you, or do you just give him what you think he wants?

A perfect example of this is the "typical" male. When his wife comes to him with a problem, his first reaction is to try and solve it when maybe all she wanted was a little of his time to vent about the problem or to talk through her solution. Wouldn't it be better to listen to her and then ask if she needs anything from you rather than to assume she wants you to solve it and give her the answer?

I have spent most of my adult life in careers where I have served other people. I believe the only true way to be successful is to help other people be successful as well.

I would encourage you to look at your life, see where you can grow, and learn to give what is needed instead of what you want to give. Together, we can make the world a place in which no one is left behind.

Robert Vance

FEAR VERSUS LOVE
Vickie Lee

I am writing this to give those who read it the courage to follow their dreams, listen to their hearts and trust their natural instincts.

For 21 years, I was a corporate "soldier," doing corporate work, making a corporate living and believing that was all there was to life. I could perform my job by rote and found the routine familiar yet numbing. I was good at what I did, but a part of me felt empty. So when my company was downsizing and asked for volunteers, I decided to leave. With much trepidation, I gave up my corporate security and said "yes" to a new life. At the same time, as fate would have it, my marriage was failing. Again, feeling as if I'd been playing a role and being unfulfilled and unhappy, I knew this, too, needed to end. Having both of my security pillars tumble simultaneously was terrifying, but I knew in my heart I had to let go in order to find peace within myself.

There I was, with two children, no job, no husband and no idea of what I would or could do with my life. This is when the magic began. I found myself being drawn to spiritual people who introduced me to the wonders of metaphysics.

I had a biofeedback therapy session and doors began to open wider. One kept leading to another, and before I knew it, I was in a turnstile of exciting and powerful, life-changing opportunities.

It started with the decision to open my own biofeedback business. Although I certainly had my apprehensions, I knew this was where my destiny was leading. Our instincts are very powerful, yet they are not as simple to follow as one might hope. It seems so much easier to give up or to continue to avoid the messages that confront us. I looked deep inside and noticed I was attracting many knowledgeable and positive connections as I researched the field. Although I knew I needed to proceed with my own feelings and ideas, I have learned there is an infinite amount of information to gather. Not all of the information was in my best interest and I learned to follow and value my own intuition. I'm finding it is kind of like building up a muscle. The more I use it, the more powerful it becomes.

The other thing I've been learning to control is my attitude. Life can be challenging at times, but I know I always have a choice. I can choose to stay positive and look on the bright side instead of being taken over with doubt. Staying positive brings joy in place of heartache and I believe it attracts more good. I was introduced to the Law of Attraction in *The Secret* and am living proof that it works.

Finding success in my biofeedback practice, I decided to expand into a full line of natural health treatments. I named my company Aqua Lea— Better Energy for Better Health—operating from the principle of quantum physics that we are all energy. I have the ability to nurture and am fascinated and gratified by the variety of therapies that help people heal themselves naturally.

I have invested in some amazing technologies, such as footbaths, that remove toxins right before your eyes. In this modern world we live in, toxins are everywhere. Even people who are diligent about what they eat and what they bring into their personal environments have been found to have toxins in their bodies. So, you can imagine what the rest of us must be dealing with on a daily basis. To be able to witness the toxins being removed and the resultant benefits reported by my clients makes me love my new found profession even more.

Another typical Aqua Lea treatment would include a relaxing session on a mat filled with amethyst. Developed by engineers, scientists and medical professionals, this simple therapy is proving to be a viable healing modality for reducing pain, stress, excess weight, toxins, fatigue and so much more. This FDA-approved medical device may be the easiest treatment yet. All you have to do is lie down on this "magic carpet" and let the energy of the amethysts do the rest. You will wake up feeling refreshed and rejuvenated!

My clients aren't the only ones who benefit from the various modalities Aqua Lea has to offer. I get to experience these treatments as well. The results have been remarkable! I've never been very good at meditating, but after just a few minutes on the BioMat mentioned before, I find myself drifting off into a peaceful, relaxing state I've never experienced before. I feel healthier than I've felt in years!

Working for myself has given me so many wonderful benefits besides just feeling healthier. I also feel more in touch with my true self, which has given me the gift of being more present for my family. The years with my children seem to fly by, and I am so grateful to be able to be here for them, enjoy them and relate to them, unhurried and heart-centered.

Another benefit is that I've been told I even look younger. I don't know if it's a result of another treatment I have learned and became certified to offer, but I'm sure it helps. I was introduced to this treatment—called Rejuvanessence—by another dear friend. After months of intensive training, I introduced this therapy into my practice to not only give my clients a more youthful appearance, but to also give them another way to totally relax. It is so gratifying to watch people look in the mirror and see what this "finger-tip facelift" can do.

For me, there is no better feeling than helping people look and feel their best. I look back at my years in the corporate world and, even though I felt I was a part of creating something useful, I don't regret for a minute the new path I chose. Stepping out in faith was not easy, but I am so grateful I did. I feel I have been guided to my true calling. My life has been enriched with new friends and kindred spirits who have led by example and encouraged me to be all that I can be.

Looking back, I can see I was motivated by fear in the form of security for those 21 years. Fear feels like running away, where love feels like running toward. Now, when I wake up, I'm excited about what my day will hold. I am so grateful to love the career I've chosen and to be moving forward with confidence that I am on the right path.

I have learned I can trust my inner guidance and have renewed my relationship with my higher source. I now pay attention when my turnstile rotates and am excited to see what new opportunity awaits. I watch the synchronicities and trust that everything happens in divine order.

Joining the Wake Up Team is stretching me again. Even though I've been told I would be good in public speaking, radio, TV and the publishing field, just the thought made me nervous and uncomfortable and, more frankly stated, it scared me half to death! But the timing of this opportunity was just too obvious to miss and I know I am ready to face more fears. Life is an exciting journey. I've learned to love putting one foot in front of the other and discovering what new gift awaits—living from my heart.

Vickie Lee

It's Never Too Late to Dream Your Dreams
Mara Diamond

"The future belongs to those who believe in the beauty of their dreams."—Eleanor Roosevelt

I remembered standing by my sister Norma's grave in Sacramento, California. I was all alone in the cemetery. The air was still—not even a breeze. I felt lonely and lost as I stood there. I looked up at the trees, hoping to see something alive, and on that day, even the birds that are often there had escaped into the silence.

I stared into the distance and suddenly, for the first time, I noticed a building. I wondered what it could be. Before I knew it, I was walking toward it. I entered and saw a long room with shelves from floor to ceiling. On the shelves were books. "What is this?" I asked myself. Then it dawned on me. What looked like books were actually containers for ashes of people who had been cremated.

I was thinking to myself that each person is the author of his or her own life. Each day of life is another page in the book. I continued to wonder if these people knew how they mattered in the fabric of life. How often do we, as humans, succumb to letting other people and circumstances write on the pages of our lives?

I just stood there thinking that each day is a new page in each life and no matter how long or how short the individual life may be, it can be an original masterpiece. Like Robert Louis Stevenson said, "To be what we are, and to become what we are capable of becoming, is the only end of life."

As a certified dream coach, I invite my clients to become dreamers—the authors of their lives. I coach and teach a remarkable process founded and written by Marcia Wieder of Dream Coach University. It is never too late to start dreaming.

I traveled to Mexico in 1967, studied yoga and was certified as an instructor by the world-famous Indra Devi, known as the first lady of yoga. At the time, she often said she would go back to India to retire, and she did just that. At the age of 86, she rekindled her passion for yoga and traveled to Argentina to open two yoga foundations. Indra Devi was still teaching yoga when she was in her 90s. She was still practicing some yoga postures at the age of 100. At 102 she quietly and peacefully passed away.

It is never too late to start dreaming. It is never too late to be the author of your own life. My purpose in life is to be of service as I inspire and empower my clients, one step at a time, to evolve and blossom into their own potential.

I had the joy of witnessing just that with Lula, a client in California. It was so exciting to see her tune into her own intention for the dream that she wanted to manifest in her life.

With her personal integrity, she rewrote the pages of her book of life by completing what was still incomplete through forgiveness. Then she was free to change anything she wanted to change. Lula found her purpose and rekindled her passion for living the life she loves. As Marcia Wieder said: "Once you know what your purpose is, you will be able to find countless ways to live on purpose. This will bring you greater joy and passion. Life will always be richer and more meaningful."

In Lula's own words, making her dreams come true means the world to her.

As a certified dream coach, I am grateful to continuously grow and to see my clients grow as well as we navigate through all the possibilities by stretching and reaching our own potential, one person at a time, becoming dreamers and living from vision rather than living from the past and repeating the same patterns over and over again.

It is never too late to dream new dreams. Each person can become the adventurer and creator of his or her own future.

Mara Diamond

How to Make a Difference in Other People's Lives
Ruben Gonzalez

There are several definitions of character. One definition is how you act when no one is looking. Another definition of character is how you treat people who could not possibly benefit you in any way. How you treat people who cannot do something for you says a lot about you. Do you ignore them? Do you walk over them or do you encourage and help them?

What difference does it make? It makes a huge difference! Character is a big part of leadership. People are more likely to follow and trust you if you are a person of character. They will also want to develop long-term relationships with you. Your whole quality of life improves when you are a person of character.

The 2002 luge season was a tough one for me. All season long, I was plagued with injuries that made it hard for me to get into any kind of good rhythm. My injuries made it hard for me to focus as much as I needed to, and consequently, my sliding was very sloppy.

I compensated by playing it safe. By taking fewer risks down the track, I didn't crash once during the regular season. That sounds like a good thing, but it really wasn't. You see, by taking safe lines down the track, my times were very slow. I needed to take more risks, especially on training runs where you have an opportunity to try out different lines to find the best ones to use on race day.

With a couple of weeks left in the season, I bet my coach that if I made it through the season and through the Olympics without crashing, he needed to buy me a new speed suit. That was a big mistake on my part. Instead of focusing on not crashing, I should have been focusing on getting better race times. As my coach agreed on the bet, he had one of those funny smiles that told me he knew something I didn't know.

Somehow, I made it through the regular season without any crashes. Now we're at the Salt Lake City Olympics. I had 10 runs to go, consisting of six training runs and the four Olympic runs. The Salt Lake track is the fastest in the world with top speeds of 85 miles per hour. The track was in unbelievable condition for the Olympics. Even though luge tracks look smooth on television, they are actually bumpy. When you're sliding, it feels like you're racing a pickup truck down a dirt road. You usually have a splitting headache after just one run, and later you must face taking several more runs.

The Salt Lake Olympic track was different. Someone told me the track workers had actually smoothed the ice with acetylene torches, making it feel like glass. I was taking my first training run and it did not even feel like the luge. I was thinking, "This feels so great...so smooth...so good...so...." Instead of focusing on how well prepared the ice was, I should have been focusing on making it down the track.

Crash!

Without any warning, I had one of the worst crashes of my career. I didn't even see it coming, so it caught me completely off guard. For the first time in my life, I was completely disoriented. I remember seeing the sky twice and hitting the bottom of the track twice. The whole time I was thinking, "Please, God, don't let me break any bones! I'm racing in the Olympics in two days!"

Luckily I didn't break anything. However, for the next two days, there was blood in my urine. It scared me to death, but I didn't dare go see the doctor because he would surely have taken me from the race. After the crash, the doctor had examined me and said that I had bruised my kidneys, but it was nothing serious.

However, my sled was a mess. The steel runners were gouged and scratched so badly I didn't think I would be able to fix them in time for the race. The medics picked me up and drove me back to the men's start house at the top of the mountain.

I walked into the start house holding my sled. My face must have been ashen because all the other athletes looked at me and starting mumbling in different languages. Then, something incredible happened. Jonathan Edwards walked right up to me, took a look at my sled, and said, "Give me 30 minutes and a file and I'll have your steels looking like new."

I didn't even know Jonathan Edwards! Jonathan had competed for the U.S. team in the 1994 Lillehammer Winter Olympics. In Salt Lake City, Jonathan was coaching the Bermuda Luge Team.

Jonathan had nothing to gain from helping me. He helped me because he had a big heart. He's a person of character who is genuinely interested in helping other people. He's just a terrific guy. Jonathan got me out of a terrible situation. He just showed up out of nowhere, like a guardian angel.

It's very unusual to find someone like that. What if we all strove to be a little bit more like Jonathan? Would we have more influence over everyone we meet? Would the world be a better place?

Character counts big time!

Ruben Gonzalez

INNER PEACE *IS* WORLD PEACE
Jessica Ardeal

Wanted: Must be available 24 hours a day, seven days a week and 365 days a year. Full-time position with overtime, no vacation, no bonuses, no sick days, no personal days and no paycheck. Interested?

Well, you are in luck. The position has already been filled, but you are not off the hook just yet. Look in the mirror. Our bodies are in service to us all day, every day, no matter what. When was the last time you gave any consideration to what goes on behind the scenes in this one place we may truly call home? When was the last time you stopped to appreciate your body and all the things it does to navigate your busy schedule? What if you put in extra-long hours at your job, day after day, and were never acknowledged for all your efforts? Is it possible your body might be feeling that way right now?

Underneath our skin (the body's largest organ) is a system of services that supports us while we work, play and even while we sleep. We rarely tend to check with our kidneys, adrenals, spleen, pancreas, liver, gall-bladder or respiratory system. In fact, you can have more productive employees if you invest the time to know them individually rather than just piling work on their desks and walking away without so much as a "thanks." We are the managers of our bodies and a little care and attention can go a long way. One definition of service is "an act of helpful activity." Our bodies help to keep us alive. Perhaps now is the time to consider some worthwhile investments for our billion dollar bodies.

Think of the body as a computer. Technology perfectly illustrates the lines of communication that are invisible to the eye. With the touch of a button, we can instantly connect to someone or something across the globe. Our body networks in the same fashion, interacting and connecting within a split second on a cellular level from head to toe. Visualize all the inner pieces—vital organs and systems—that add up to equal the whole, magnificent person you are.

There are more than 6,000 languages on record around the world, but there is one language we have overlooked. The universal language of the body is a language in which we all have the capacity to become fluent. Did you ever notice that your body has your complete attention when it signals you through an ache, pain or illness? Signals are how our bodies communicate to us that something needs to be acknowledged or addressed. All too often we silence, rather than explore, their meanings. Perhaps something is being lost in translation? There is, I believe, a way to connect with these inner pieces—organs and systems—so we can feel our inner peace. Our bodies possess an infinite wisdom and with access to this innate intelligence, we can exponentially raise consciousness across the planet.

When you hear the words "inner peace is world peace," what comes to mind? Do the words resonate with you? In essence, your world is what you see immediately in front of you. Sure, there are over six billion people on the planet, but how many of them do you know personally? Your inner peace is your world peace and it can be that simple. We have been exploring everything outside of ourselves for centuries, expecting to find the answers to the great mysteries of life. Still, amidst the advances and luxuries of modern society, the inner space of the human body remains a mystery. This is illustrated by television shows such as *Mystery ER*, *Mystery Diagnosis*, *Diagnosis Unknown*, *Diagnosis X* and others. When we develop a greater understanding and appreciation for the inner pieces—organs and systems—and when we go below the surface of what we see, a new world emerges and a deeper compassion for humanity can exist.

We are here in this world to co-create. Each one of us has a part in creating the world we live in. In everyday transactions, there is a give and take, an offering and receiving. We each have our own unique talents and gifts and a body that helps fulfill our divine purpose. Some of us may find ourselves doing jobs we don't enjoy, living paycheck to paycheck and complaining about the way the world works. When was the last time you heard someone say, "Yay! I get to be of service today!"? Can you imagine waking up every morning with that thought?

Everything in this world began with a thought, a spark of energy sent from the brain to the body and manifested in our tangible reality. Energy powers everything, from home and office conveniences to vehicles. You can have a full tank of gas, but you are not getting out of the driveway with a dead battery. We are, essentially, energy in human form. What is your energy level? Do you feel powerless or empowered? We don't see energy, but we do see the effects of energy. If a lamp is unplugged, you can flip the switch for as long as you would like, but until you put the cord into the outlet and make the connection, it will remain dark. You must connect with your inner pieces to illuminate your power. The essence of a happy life is a light spirit, a joyful and grateful heart and a conscious body-mind connection. The next time you are in line at the grocery store, at the movies, stuck in traffic or wherever you find yourself feeling frustrated or impatient, take a deep breath and be at peace. Stop to consider the fact that scientific research determined we are a staggering 99.97 percent the same, genetically. Consider the inner pieces—organs and systems—of those around you. Rather than making idle chit-chat about the weather, engage each others' thyroids, stomachs or hearts; consider the pineal and pituitary of the person next to you.

We have more in common than we realize. There is always more than meets the eye. What you get is what you see. Get in front of your mirror. Give thanks for your body working non-stop, all day, every day. If you find yourself hanging onto your perceived imperfections, take the word "imperfect" and change it to "I'm perfect." Repeat to yourself, "I'm perfect the way I am, I am perfection in human form." Rather than thinking about what is wrong with your body, realize how perfectly it is working for your survival and recognize the beauty within. Have patience with yourself and enjoy your journey. Always be true to who you are and be present in every moment. Honor your body as well as your talents, insights, hopes and desires. What we imagine can be our new reality. All you have to do is live the life you love, love the body you are in and nature will take care of the rest. The sooner we all do this and feel our inner peace, the sooner we will see a world of peace.

Jessica Ardeal

EMBRACE SILENCE
Dr. Wayne W. Dyer®

You live in a noisy world, constantly bombarded with loud music, sirens, construction equipment, jet airplanes, rumbling trucks, leaf blowers, lawn mowers and tree cutters. These manmade, unnatural sounds invade your senses and keep silence at bay.

In fact, you've been raised in a culture that not only eschews silence, but is terrified of it. The car radio must always be on, and any pause in conversation is a moment of embarrassment that most people quickly fill with chatter. For many, being alone in silence is pure torture.

The famous scientist Blaise Pascal observed, "All man's miseries derive from not being able to sit quietly in a room alone."

With practice, you can become aware that there's a momentary silence in the space between your thoughts. In this silent space, you'll find the peace that you crave in your daily life. You'll never know that peace if you don't have any spaces between your thoughts.

The average person is said to have 60,000 separate thoughts a day. With so many thoughts, there are almost no gaps. If you could reduce that number by half, you would open up an entire world of possibilities for yourself. For it is when you merge into the silence, and become one with it, that you reconnect to your source and know the peacefulness that some call "God." It is stated beautifully in Psalms of the Old Testament: "Be still and know that I am God." The key words are "still" and "know."

"Still" actually means "silence." Mother Teresa described silence and its relationship to God by saying, "God is the friend of silence. See how nature (trees, grass) grows in silence. We need silence to be able to touch souls." This includes your soul.

It's really the space between the notes that make the music you enjoy so much. Without the spaces, all you would have is one continuous, noisy note. Everything that's created comes out of silence. Your thoughts emerge from the nothingness of silence. Your words come out of this void. Your very essence emerged from emptiness.

All creativity requires some stillness. Your sense of inner peace depends on spending some of your life energy in silence to recharge your batteries, removing tension and anxiety, thus reacquainting you with the joy of knowing God and feeling closer to all of humanity. Silence reduces fatigue and allows you to experience your own creative juices.

The second word in the Old Testament observation, "know," refers to making your personal and conscious contact with God. To know God is to banish doubt and become independent of others' definitions and descriptions of God. Instead, you have your own personal knowing. And, as Melville reminded us so poignantly, "God's one and only voice is silence."

Dr. Wayne W. Dyer®

GIVING BACK
Kandi A. White

So how does a small island girl from Bermuda get the opportunity to be a co-author in the best-selling series *Wake Up…Live the Life You Love*? I'm not going to reveal that answer just yet. Hopefully, before you finish reading this chapter, you'll understand. Let me just tell you, I'm truly blessed and grateful to be able to share a little about my journey with you.

In February of 2003, while in pursuit to become one of the top five percent most successful Internet marketers and to create financial independence to live the life I desired, I was transformed.

At a leadership seminar, I came face-to-face with God and the real me. In the twinkling of an eye and the snap of a finger, I had a life-changing experience. It was the defining moment in my life. My true purpose was revealed, and I am now truly living the life I love.

This life no longer consists of seeking my own fulfillment, but is a life of service to God and to the people with whom I am fortunate to have a relationship. All my life I considered myself a Christian, having been brought up in Sunday school and church. In 1976, at the age of 14, I accepted Jesus as my savior during a week-long Young Life teen camp. I began to understand what being a follower of Jesus really meant.

During my early adult years, my Christian life continued to grow. I truly appreciated all the challenges that God helped me through, and I had many achievements in both my professional and personal life. Yet, I didn't allow God to be in charge of every aspect of my life. It wasn't until I was at the leadership seminar listening to Dr. Wayne W. Dyer® that I had a "wake-up" moment.

Words cannot explain how desperate I had been to attend the seminar. It still amazes me that I had one goal in mind while God had another.

God put certain people in my direct path to "wake me up" and to let me know that I needed to make changes in the path I was following. I will be forever grateful for Dr. Wayne W. Dyer®, Mr. Jim Rohn, Mr. Les Brown and the other remarkable speakers for being God's messengers during the weekend that changed my life.

I realized that I allowed God to take charge of my church, my prayer life and my Sunday school involvement. He could lead and direct me in these areas with full control. The other side of my personal life, the friends I had, the places I traveled, the Internet marketing businesses I got involved in—anything outside of my church life—I didn't allow God to be in charge. Sometimes, as Christians, we think we can hide our sinful ways from God and keep them a secret. We can't hide anything from God. He knows our coming and our going and, best of all, He knows what is in our hearts.

Even before leaving the seminar, I knew I was going to make some drastic changes. I knew my life was going to take a new path. I decided at that very moment I would write a book about my weekend experience and the gratitude I felt. I wanted others to get a glimpse of just how powerful God is and to be motivated by the real life success stories of the seminar speakers. The information was powerful and I could not keep it to myself.

In 2004, I finished writing and self-publishing *Hours of Pure Gold*, a book of inspiration, motivation and gratitude. The process took several months and many late nights, but I was determined because my transformation story was written within its pages.

Since 2003, my focus has changed, as well as my life purpose. I've learned to listen to the still, small voice of the Holy Spirit as He guides me in all that I do. I know Jesus walks beside me.

I'm inspired by people who are motivated to help others reach their purpose. They motivate and inspire me to share my gifts and talents because of all the blessings I've received. It's no longer about me. It's about God's purpose for my life and serving others through community service and *Hours of Pure Gold*.

Each month, in the *Hours of Pure Gold* newsletter, I write an article on inspiration, motivation or gratitude. I encourage others to find their true purpose and to never give up on achieving their goals. I could not do this without God's help and guidance. I would give up too easily in my own strength. There are subscribers from around the world and I enjoy telling them that Jesus loves them and is there for them in everything they do.

God never stops giving me creative ideas. As these ideas become tangible projects, books, Web sites, journals, businesses, trusts and inventions, I will forever be thankful for the transformation of my life.

After I finished writing the book, God placed on my heart the desire to write a manuscript for a kid's journal. This beautiful journal will contain prayers, poems, quotes, words of encouragement and favorite scripture promises for young children. This journal idea came to me from Jim Rohn, whose journal I purchased. Our young people need to write about their dreams, aspirations and what they are thankful for. The prayers and quotes will enforce just how special they are and they will know there's nothing they cannot accomplish.

I also love Internet marketing and involve myself in businesses that are wholesome and those in which the leaders care for people and want to help make others' lives better. Teamwork is important and I enjoy working with my team.

Each day when I wake, I thank God for the new day, I invite the Holy Spirit to dwell in my heart and I ask Jesus to help me see people through His eyes and to love them as He loves them. This is what gets me up in the morning.

As we humble ourselves daily, seek to know God by reading His word. By having faith, God will open doors that are beyond our comprehension. He will fill our hearts with pure joy and give us inner peace.

I surrendered my life and everything I have to God and He gives me purpose. That's how a small island girl gets to co-author in a best-selling series *Wake Up... Live the Life You Love.*

You have a purpose, too!

Kandi A. White

Queen of Breath, To My Dearest Mother, Clara!
M. Rose Windels

Beloved Mom, you were my pride, my friend, my master and my student. Yes, you were my greatest and best student and you made me a great master!

After returning from my South African tour, the first thing I did was visit my mom.

"You look gorgeous," she said with a smile in her eyes. "But I want to go now!"

"Where do you want to go, Mom?" I asked her as if I did not know.

Her face was black and blue. She had fallen out of her chair again. After a bout with dementia and Alzheimer's, I told her she could transition another way. She listened to my solution and replied, "Remember, you told me once how I could step out of this life without pain and you promised me I could count on you to help me? Is that still so?"

My heart clenched in a knot. I knew she was serious this time. The sweat ran off my forehead and mingled with the tears forming up behind my eyelids. I shook my head like a cat, trying to clear my ears. Did I hear correctly? She was serious and at peace with it. Her look was tender and her face glowed.

Having to let her go made me nauseous. The love I felt for that beautiful woman, my precious mother, was and still is so big, enormous and vulnerable.

"Yes, Mom. I am here to help you. Your wish is my command." My voice was thin and shaky. I didn't want to hold her back this time! Three times I brought her back to life. Three times I wasn't ready to let her go.

The 14th of February was our yearly Champagne Day. Not the only one in the year. Our Valentine's Day's brand of champagne was Demoiselle because we are "demoiselles," which is French for "girls." This made it a very significant day.

We toasted and Mom sipped some drops of pink, sparkling nectar from her glass. She shook her head to give me the hint. It's enough. Like lovers, we held hands throughout the day and the night. I wanted so much to be with her, comfort her and mother her, for this would be a delicate parting of ways.

Very slowly, she desired less and less food and water. I had decided and promised her I would stay with her the last two weeks of her life.

The last two days, a sudden miracle happened. She started conscious breathing, rebirthing, the daily vitamin breathe-work I taught the nurses to practice with her.

Fourteen years ago, I showed her how to rebirth in order to breathe herself back into life when a stroke partially paralyzed her body. The breathe-work had popped her back into life and gave her 14 years of good health.

Now was the real time. She went from session to session, said a one-liner and breathed. While one of the trainees passed by, Mom begged her to breastfeed her baby. Sandy, confused, asked, "How do you know I am pregnant, Clara?" Meanwhile, Mom went on to her next session and stuck to her breathing.

I felt so proud of her and so proud of myself. I taught her how to rebirth and she did not forget. I held her beautiful, tiny, skinny hands as porcelain in my own. Her whole being went transparent as if she turned into a light being. Our energies cross fired and built a bond forever. I took her in my arms and told her it was time to take care and to let go.

"I am big enough now, Mom. I can take care of myself. I am ready to let you go!"

Suddenly, she pulled herself up and, with an almost inaudible tiny voice, said, "My mother was here. She told me it is so beautiful where she is!"

My whole being felt an overwhelming sense of gratitude toward the grandmother I had never known. The tangible vibration in the room buzzed and other family members had questioning looks in their eyes. They felt something very special was happening, something they couldn't or didn't want to understand.

Meanwhile, Mom's body turned blue. I saw the life going out of the top of her head. I called my brother, sisters, nieces, nephews and all the nurses. Therese, my beloved sister from South Africa, flew in to be with our mom.

My niece, Veerle, and my brother stood the closest to her. Ivan, at the end of the bed, looked fearfully at Mom while she held her head up and looked him straight in the face and said with relief in her voice, "Iban," which is Portuguese for Ivan. He was married to a Portuguese woman. Was that a last vitamin-humor?

Mom laid down again and started breathing all over again.

Her hand searched for a tighter grip. She turned her face to me and said, "I hear noises! Is it raining? I am afraid now!" Her grip still tighter, "What is going to happen? Where am I going?"

I stepped a little closer to her to catch the intimacy between us and said, "Maatje, it is not raining. Can you accept your fear and try to let it go, as in 'I let go!'"?

I could not believe my ears when I heard her breathe in on the "I let go" and breathe out on the "I let go!" Where did she get this spontaneous rhythmical breath song?

My whole family looked at me for an explanation. I had none. That was the "here and now" of my mom's passing away. Mom, in transition, gave me—a rebirther—the greatest honor by breathing herself to the other side.

There was togetherness with the whole family that I'd never experienced before. Maatje got the love of all of us to go where she wanted so much to go.

"Maatje," I said. "Please let me know when you arrive."

She nodded and said angelically, "I am not afraid anymore." She sighed a very deep sigh and suddenly screamed one big yell. We all had goose bumps. Every hair on my head stood up. Veerle, my niece, was frightened. She looked at me and asked, "What was that?"

I knew she had let go. Her hand lay softly in mine. The scream was the moment that her spirit left her body.

In early February of this year, I was sitting at my desk writing this story when I noticed myself staring at one big red flower on Mom's hibiscus.

I then knew it was a sign: Mom had arrived!

Thank you, "Maatje," for keeping your promise.

> You did all the good you could,
> With the tools you had,
> The way you knew,
> On the place you lived,
> In the time given to you,
> For all of us you've loved.

M. Rose Windels

MANIFESTING MATISSE
Dr. Michelle Nielsen

Nearly five years after my son's traumatic premature birth, I sat across from his teacher with my fingers nervously knotting together and my heart racing. "We're very concerned about Matisse," she said. "He's not speaking. He's still acting like a baby. If we don't see significant improvement by spring, we're going to have to help you find a school for children like him."

I had been living in a dream—a dream in which my son was fine. Sure, he had a few problems. He had "special needs" (a term that, ironically, had secured him a seat in that prestigious school in the first place). Still, he was fine.

Like a baby!
In the space of a second, I found myself reliving the last minutes of my pregnancy and the first months of Matisse's life. Ambulances. Hospitals. A "fetus" not expected to survive. A tiny, teacup-sized baby, weighing just 1.5 pounds. He was small enough to be held in one hand, but too fragile to be held. There were tubes, monitors, needles, chilly sensors and a cold, sterile incubator, along with months of isolation from almost all human touch. The doctor's voice said, "Be prepared for a child who is developmentally delayed—perhaps severely." I spent years in denial.

Yes, I had been living in a dream, but now I was awake—fully awake. I could no longer pretend my son was fine. I started crying uncontrollably, to the teacher's embarrassment. After a few minutes, I managed to calm myself, put on my sunglasses to hide my red eyes and headed home.

Once there, I found my way to the terrace and sat down for my daily meditation. After a few minutes, the pain in my heart eased. My anxieties and fears melted away in the comforting silence. Inspiration arrived in the form of a thrilling possibility I'd never before considered. Could I take a leap of faith and act on it? I could!

When I opened my eyes, Matisse's situation was unchanged, but I was a different person. "This is not going to be!" I thought with determination and something like joy. "Matisse will be a healthy, normally developing little boy!"

The facts were grim. While his classmates were chattering away, Matisse's vocabulary consisted of just six words strangled by a painful stutter: "Mi-mi-mi-mi-mi-mi-milk!" He could not complete even the most basic exercises in school and extensive testing showed his developmental delays were, in fact, severe. Therapists warned us his permanent neurological damage meant he might never be able to speak or even smile normally.

So why was I able to take a leap of faith and believe my son could be healed in so little time? A lifetime of experience.

Thanks to early training in the Silva Ultra-Mind Method, and the fact that I had many free hours on my hands, I began experimenting with reality as a small child. When my experiments were successful, I decided to use what I'd learned to escape poverty—and I did—even before I actually left home.

Throughout my adolescent years, money and resources flowed to me almost effortlessly. I always had cash on hand for clothes, lessons and other extras our family could not afford. "Michelle is rich!" my sister would tell her friends, proudly and with a bit of envy. I let her words feed my ego. I did not recognize within them the opportunity to use my skills to help her. I am sad to say this blindness persisted well into my 30s.

By now, the principles I used and still use today are probably no secret to you. They're founded on the laws of quantum physics made famous in recent years through the hit films *What the Bleep Do We Know?* and *The Secret*. Using them, I manifested success, affluence and personal achievement as an adult. From the wealth they created, I gave generously to meaningful causes, but I never considered using what I'd learned in direct service to another human being until the day the words of my son's teacher shook me awake. After that, I wasted no time.

Less than an hour after our conversation, I began applying my thoughts, emotions and energy toward my son's healing. Miracles began to occur. Within days, Matisse's stutter began to fade. His vocabulary started to grow rapidly—often increasing by as many as two or three words between our walk to school in the morning and his bedtime story. Within three months, his stutter disappeared. Within six months, he was a certifiable chatterbox, gabbing away confidently in three languages (English, Spanish and Catalan) at every opportunity.

One year after that first, fateful meeting, Matisse has been tested and found to be developmentally appropriate, or even advanced for his age, across all areas. The "special-needs" designation that won him a place in his prestigious school has been removed. He is an avid learner and leader among his peers, and just days ago, his teacher assured us he is performing at an above average in his class.

A river of gratitude flows out of my heart for the transformation that has occurred in his life. So what could be almost as precious to me as my son's healing? The awakening that made it possible and opened my eyes to my highest purpose: *service*. I now see my reality-transformation skills as tools for effecting meaningful change in others' lives and meeting the needs of the world as a whole.

Manifesting a new car or home can be *exciting*. Manifesting a hit single or a popular consumer product can be *electrifying*. These and other similar visions are worthwhile and wonderful in and of themselves. They can give us the opportunity to take good care of ourselves and our families while we express our gifts and talents in creative and highly satisfying ways.

But what about healing for people we know? Or resources for needy and struggling people in our communities? Clean water for families everywhere? An end to global warming? Manifesting these visions is for the deeper work of the soul and it is beautiful and fulfilling beyond words.

People all over the world are in the process of discovering the greater potential of the truths now gaining a prominent place in our collective consciousness. We have the opportunity to manifest worldwide abundance, to rescue our brothers and sisters across the globe from poverty and despair. We have the opportunity to restore our planet to clean, vibrant health and balance. I believe we will.

But every bit as important as the great visions we will manifest are the *people* we will become in the process. We will manifest ourselves as we were truly meant to be—vessels through which love flows to heal the world.

Dr. Michelle Nielsen

LIFE REALLY BEGINS AT AGE 60
Rino Solberg

I was born in 1944 in Horten, a small Norwegian town. My father died in an accident when I was two years old and since 10 years of age, I have always had a job and supported myself. In 1963, I enrolled in the Air Force and took five years of engineering education until I dropped it in 1968 and my lifetime journey as an entrepreneur began. I had an electric shop when my life changed drastically in 1970 when I started working part-time as a distributor in a so-called MLM company—the first one in Norway. The personal development I went through in that company opened my eyes to the fact that "you become what you think about."

After winning a sales competition, I became the first European member of "The Eagle Club" and I received a book called *Think and Grow Rich* by Napoleon Hill. The book was dynamite. After working with this company for a couple of years, I became the first MLM person in Norway to earn an average Norwegian yearly salary every month in 1972 and became the lead training instructor in Norway.

I was now ready for bigger challenges.

I then invented the Unislip, a grinding machine for gate valves and got patents in 12 countries on my machine. After building companies in Norway, the United States, Germany and Japan, and with agents in 20 more countries, I sold the company after running it successfully for 13 years.

At that time, I wanted to get back to personal development again to motivate other people. I wanted to do that because while doing business in the United States, I met W. Clement Stone, who became my mentor and friend for more than 16 years. I also became friends with Earl Nightingale and Lloyd Conant and bought every educational and motivational tape they produced.

Through my friend W. Clement Stone, I got the idea of starting *Success* magazine in Norway. After one year, with a lot of expenses and almost no income, the company went bankrupt. I lost a lot of money and our new 550-square meter home in the process. My biggest failure, therefore, is called *Success*, and on top of that, the company itself was called Success Unlimited. I will never forget when I met W. Clement Stone after this failure and he asked me, "How is the *Success* magazine doing in Norway?" My answer was, "It went bankrupt last month." Within a fraction of a second, he shouted, loudly, "That is good!" With a softer voice he added, "Now we just have to find out what was good about it." That was positive thinking at its best and it taught me a lesson.

My wife and I attended six Napoleon Hill Gold Medal award dinners in the United States through the years. We met many great people there who were awarded the Napoleon Hill Gold Medal.

Thanks to Napoleon Hill, W. Clement Stone, Earl Nightingale, Zig Ziglar, Norman Vincent Peale, Robert Schuller, Brian Tracy, Tony Robbins and Denis Waitley, to mention a few, I learned a lot.

Now it is my time to give something back to the world in order to continue the Napoleon Hill Foundation's vision and my passion: "To make this world a better place to live, for this and future generations."

For 35 years, I have given more than 700 training courses and seminars, written nine books, published two magazines, built 22 companies in many countries (five went bankrupt), had four major financial failures, went personally bankrupt once (I was probably a slow, but eventually good, learner), have been both rich and poor, traveled to more than 30 countries and gone through two divorces. I still believe I have lived a wonderful and rich life because everything is possible with positive thinking and persistence.

However, at 60 years of age, I wanted to do something more with the rest of my life than just business (hopefully for 40 more years), something that was much bigger than me and something that could change the world—and I really found it, so let me tell you about it.

My wonderful wife, Julie, who I met in Norway in 1977, was born in Africa. We had traveled to Kenya and Uganda since 1979 and done work there since 1991 when we started an NGO called Child Africa to help children through school. In 1994, we were personally invited by the President of Uganda, Yoweri Museveni, who we met in Norway, to start quality management training in Uganda. We accepted and pioneered ISO 9000 training in Uganda and helped approximately 100 companies become certified to ISO 9000 series quality management standards. All these years working in Africa and seeing the poverty and struggle of the people there got us to begin thinking about how we could use all the knowledge and skills we had to make life better for all the poor African people.

Therefore, the decision was made. After two years of research, we started the Better Globe Group in 2006 with the vision that we would do more to eradicate poverty in Africa over the next 20 years than any other single organization has ever done.

We don't believe in charity, except during catastrophes, but we do believe strongly in "self" help and will support poor people in Africa based on principles of entrepreneurship. This will allow them to be self-sustained and able to work themselves out of poverty. We will do this by focusing our support in the following three main areas:

1. Massive Tree Planting
Without massive forestation in Africa in the next 20 to 30 years, all land suitable for farming will be gone and, consequently, so will the farmers. Massive tree planting will also hinder desertification and global warming, which is one of the biggest threats in our world today.

Goal: We are going to plant five billion trees in Africa by the year 2026.

2. Microfinance for Agriculture

Eighty percent of the people in Africa are poor farmers. Most of them survive on less than one dollar a day. If we are ever going to eradicate poverty in Africa, we have to help the poor farmers make more money for themselves through entrepreneurial approaches.

Goal: We aim to become the biggest "microfinance bank" for poor farmers in Africa by the year 2026.

3. Education of Children

If children in Africa don't have access to free primary schools, there is no way any African country will be able to eradicate poverty. We also know that poverty and corruption are closely related, so we will teach children in the schools and universities the importance of having integrity in order to fight corruption and poverty. We will offer an e-book version of my book, *Put Integrity First,* free to students in schools and universities in all the African countries as a tool to fight corruption.

Goal: We will build more schools in Africa by the year 2026 (through the NGO "Child Africa") than any other organization has ever done.

It has been said that nothing is impossible, it only takes more time. I agree with that, but I have added, "The one who attempts the impossible also has very little competition." We know that in order to succeed in our mission and to get enough good people to help us, we need to start a movement with millions of people who are able to enjoy working with our projects and, in the process, make money for a living. We have already made that possible.

There is no better way to live the life you love while making a lasting legacy, than by helping change the world and make it a better place. You can do it, too, when you find your passion.

Rino Solberg

LISTENING FOR GOD (FROM THE WAKE UP LIVE MOVIE)
Zachary Levi

My "Wake Up Moment" was when I realized how much God loved me and that there were things in my life that I wanted to do and things I felt like God had made me do. He wasn't keeping things from me because he was mad at me, he was keeping them from me because he knew that I wasn't ready for them. When I realized that, and when I realized that he wanted to bless me with those things, and I was getting my life together, then it all started falling into place. And so, my "Wake Up Moment" was knowing God's love.

So I would just tell young professionals of any kind to make sure you know why you want it. Is it because you really love the art of it, is it because you're really into the fame and the fortune? Know your motives as best you can, and know your passions as best as you can. If you are really passionate about it, you will go forward and succeed. You know, it's almost not even a choice.

So, it's not as if you're asking, "Should I be an actor?" It's "I have to be an actor, or a musician," or whatever the case may be.

But you also have to know that this may not be what you are ultimately supposed to do. Maybe it's just something you're supposed to pursue for a time that will bring you somewhere else. It should never be about who you are. It doesn't define you. You could go off to be the next Wolfgang Puck, but you never would have found that if you hadn't come to Hollywood and tried to be an actor. So always be open to wherever God is taking you.

Zachary Levi

BELIEVING IN HAPPINESS
Dr. Anne Curtis

From very early on in life I wanted to be and do something special. However, I didn't realize I was already special; I believed I had to work very hard at it. I didn't yet know the real secret to success and happiness. When I was eight, my father's childhood friend died from cancer. He was 30 years old and left three young children and many sad friends and family. His death made a big impression on me.

My father became very unhappy and my parents' relationship suffered. I did a lot of reading to escape the atmosphere at home. I loved reading, despite being dyslexic, and read about people who did special things. At age 10, I read about Louis Pasteur and decided I'd be a great scientist like him someday and would discover a cure for cancer.

I spent my teenage years studying hard, rarely allowing myself to have fun. I believed God wouldn't allow me to succeed if I didn't work every possible moment. I didn't know then that learning and life are much easier when you're enjoying yourself.

At age 16, a teacher asked if I had ever thought about being a doctor. I hadn't, but when everyone told me it was too hard to get into medical school, especially for girls, I became determined to go. I still believed everything was possible, but nothing was easy. I studied even harder, sometimes taking exams twice to get the grades I needed.

I got into medical school and loathed it. British medical students and doctors, at that time, worked ridiculously long hours in very stressful conditions, often bullied and humiliated rather than supported by their colleagues.

I was unhappy and confused. I felt trapped. I didn't know where to go or what to do, so I stayed in the system, studied even harder and got my degree. My new title qualified me to work more than 100 hours a week with little support and the responsibility of holding the fate of people's lives in my hands, but I had no time to give them real human care and attention.

I was exhausted. I knew there had to be more to life than working and coming home tired, frustrated and sad about all the people I had been unable to help.

My personal life wasn't great either. I got married, but had no idea how to have a happy relationship. I was soon divorced. Nothing seemed right. I blamed my parents, my husband and people I worked with for my lack of success, not realizing I had the power to change everything.

Out of desperation, I started asking what I could do. I received the answers out of nowhere!

I found myself in a practice in which the doctors believed all medical problems were based on the patient's emotional needs. This was a revelation and a relief. At last, I was dealing with real people! I finally started to enjoy my work.

I still believed I had to work hard, so I received further training in sexual therapy, relationship therapy and conventional psychotherapy, but the results came too slowly.

Four years after my marriage ended, I was still no closer to having a great relationship despite my own weekly therapy sessions.

Again, I wondered where I could discover methods that would work quickly and effectively to help both myself and my patients. I was soon offered a place in a wonderful NLP training. That training revolutionized my life.

Three weeks after the training ended, I married for the second time. I definitely wouldn't recommend marrying so quickly, but I learned how easy it is to manifest the things you want and how to make your "manifesting life list" infallible!

I also discovered why I'd never achieved the success or happiness I had craved: I had piles of hidden unsupportive beliefs blocking me. I went on a quest to root out all of the blocks to wealth, health, love, success and happiness.

I was so determined to be happy and successful that I spent a lot of money searching for and finding solutions. At first, I went into major debt while exploring every possibility, but I knew there had to be an answer.

Despite the money issue, I had a great time. I enjoyed my work, met and worked with hundreds of people who inspired and helped me and discovered many powerful techniques for change, including EFT, GOLD counseling and QiGong, as well as developing a few of my own along the way.

I finally discovered what works and learned to let go of the past, have endless energy, have confidence in myself, enjoy life and succeed. My life got better and better. I paid off my debts, stopped losing the money I had worked so hard to make and started making lots more.

I learned to love myself and my body and stopped putting up with being second best. I looked and felt more attractive and attracted great friends, better relationships with my family and lots of love.

For years I had told myself that money wasn't important. I believed I didn't deserve to be wealthy and was afraid people wouldn't like me if I was. I realized how wrong I had been when I found myself madly in love at last, but unable to live happily with my lover because of financial constraints. I changed that belief right away!

I now know money can be a huge benefit in a loving relationship, providing a comfortable place to live, more time to have fun and peace of mind. At last, I know money is a good thing, though it took a while!

I have often heard people say they would rather have good health than lots of money. However, I have patients who could have much better health if they could afford the best foods, supplements and therapies available. Why choose between the two when it's better and possible to have it all?

Although I took the hard road, I learned so much. I learned you don't need to work hard or have qualifications to succeed and be happy. In fact, those things can sometimes get in the way!

At first glance, it might seem that doctors, lawyers and other professionals who've studied and worked hard are successful, but most professionals I know—those who make a pretty good income—are overworked, unhappy, dissatisfied and stuck working hard to maintain their lifestyles, while longing for more energy, time, love, fun, fulfillment and happiness.

Of course, I still work hard when I choose to, but instead of working horrendous hours feeling stressed and unhappy, I do only what I love in beautiful, peaceful surroundings. I choose to pass on all I've learned about how to have and enjoy great health and real wealth, true happiness and love—easily!

Dr. Anne Curtis

PASSIONATE ABOUT CHILDREN
Sandi Schwartz

I am leading a gentle, loving revolution, changing the way Americans think about the next generation. I am stirring a flame in the hearts of parents, encouraging them to seek the wisdom, understanding and skills that will make a difference in the way they live life with their children. Parents are tired of yelling, punishing and getting angry and frustrated. They are ready to make the shift into authentic love and outrageous joy. I believe I was born to lead the way into this new state of consciousness.

My life's passion was etched in my heart at the age of two when my father walked out of my life. I never saw him again. I lived in the shadow of my parents' anger and pain, too young to know this event would be the catalyst of a divine spark that would morph into a life of service to future generations.

It was the late 1940s. Divorce was a shameful concept that was spoken about mostly through whispers and rumors. My mom and I moved into her parents' home and my father's disappearance was never discussed. Though it was never said to me directly, I knew I was not to bring up the subject, so I lived my childhood pretending not to notice that I was the only one in my neighborhood who didn't have a daddy.

Growing up, I received a lot of love and nurturing. But in this love there was an unspoken expectation. I was to listen to the adults, do my homework, practice the piano, be a good little girl and always appear happy and content. If I fulfilled my part of this non-verbal agreement, Mommy and Grandma would reward me with smiles and praise. Thus, I learned to rely on a false sense of security. I lived with the fear that if I displeased them they might abandon me and I would be alone in the world.

It was not until many years later that I realized I had spent my childhood denying my own truths. Unconsciously, I stuffed my feelings, needs and questions deep down inside my heart in order to guarantee my place as the "good girl." I chose the protection of pretending to be happy over dealing with the anger and pain I feared would be released if I stepped out of these prescribed behaviors. I was a good girl. I had to be, it kept me safe.

With every fiber of my being, I believe I came into this life to be that little girl and to grow into this woman of purpose and passion. I brought with me a divine consciousness that had to lie dormant while I experienced a childhood of conditional love. I know the difference between being a victim and experiencing victory is how we choose to look at what happens in our lives and the key to a life of fulfillment is turning sadness into genuine, authentic purpose. With the hindsight of decades of growth, I have come to appreciate my childhood and the way it influenced my life's work. I became a teenager determined to change the world. I became a teacher. I became a wife. I became a parent. I became a director of children's programs. I became a college instructor. I became a motivational speaker. I became a consultant. I became an author. I became an expert.

This was all external to me. These were my labels. This was how the world saw me and it was what gave me clout, respect and status. It continued to keep me safe. While I was achieving outward success, the little girl who lived inside me was kicking, screaming and pushing me to be brave enough to find out who I really was. I stopped ignoring her tantrums and began to listen. I discovered a tiny inner voice that was trying to get my attention.

Thus began a journey toward inner knowing and discovering my buried truths. As I let go of the fear of connecting with my deeper self, I found the courage to stop pleasing other people. Through my expanding spiritual awareness, I eventually came to trust the wisdom of my own soul. This process of growth is ongoing. There are still moments when I might lose myself to the opinions of others rather than following my own inner guidance, but I remain committed to living life with an open, truthful heart and an uncompromising passion.

This journey has led me to interview hundreds of adults, asking them about their early years and how their childhood experiences continue to impact them today. Many of these people are looking for a coach or mentor who will help them reclaim their dignity and self-respect. They are painfully aware that, somewhere along the way, they lost the natural and joyful gifts with which they were born. I have become the loving warrior on a mission to teach parents how to live in a way that encourages their children to make responsible choices while remaining eager, free-spirited and open to the beauty of life.

My "call to revolution" begins with a plea to all the adults whose lives impact the world of a child. I encourage you to open your mind, heart and soul with a willingness to embrace a shift in thinking and being. This new world includes learning to trust your intuition, listening to the inner source that lives within us all and being brave and fearless in pronouncing that your children—each and every one of them—have a gift to bring to this world. Each child has his or her own unique brand of intelligence, talent and creativity. Each and every child deserves to sparkle and expand in a joyful environment that supports individual greatness. Our goal as parents and teachers should be to help them learn to listen to their own internal wisdom.

I imagine homes across America in which parents and grandparents change their expectations for their children from pleasing others to following their dreams and from simply listening to the advice of the adults to having adult role models who embrace life fearlessly and powerfully.

I dream of a world in which children no longer need to "be good" or get top grades in order for their parents to feel they are successful. Instead of convincing children they need Mom or Dad to make important decisions, we can teach them to listen to their innate sense of knowledge and the messages of their body and heart. Genius and leadership blossom more powerfully with inspired thought guided from inner harmony. This new way of thinking may make parents uncomfortable at first, but they, too, will benefit from the flow of energy and vitality that will enrich their lives as they release the "old world" belief systems that keep them unconsciously stuck in their own childhood pain.

Changing existing paradigms includes giving parents the skills to encourage their children to be caring, responsible, freedom-seeking lovers of life. I envision parents forgiving themselves and their own parents for past mistakes. I see the older generations becoming role models of gratitude and appreciation, daring to live life free of gossip, anger, frustration, hurt, guilt and worry.

It is my greatest desire and deepest passion to create this dramatic change in the way we think about raising children. As a parent and educator, I have seen children embrace empathetic, sensitive, happy, successful and cooperative behavior without the threat of punishment, time-outs or physical and emotional hurt. It can be done!

There is magic in the air. There is a vibration of powerful love and authentic happiness pulsating across our land. There are little children giggling, joyfully anticipating a life of adventure and growth. There are moments of intense satisfaction just waiting to be enjoyed by the little ones and their families. I am sending out an invitation to everyone reading this book to be part of this loving revolution.

Is it possible that the child who lives inside of you needs to be heard? Is there a passion, a desire to serve, a shift in consciousness that is stirring in your soul? As you move through your day, you may want to quiet your mind and begin to feel the awakening that is coming through you. Personal fulfillment, aliveness and creativity are waiting for us all.

What is your inner voice telling you?

Sandi Schwartz

SUCCESS: HELPING OTHERS SUCCEED AND GROW
Gregory Scott Reid

It has been said that the sign of a life well lived is one that was spent serving others. Let's face it, would you get more enjoyment from getting a pat on the back at work or watching someone you helped to excel get the same kudos in the cubicle next to you? It seems that when we focus our attention toward the betterment of others, we get the same amount of appreciation in return.

It may not always be vocalized, but internal satisfaction is something that cannot be bottled or sold. It's the same feeling of pride parents feel when their child rides his bike for the first time without training wheels, or when he later graduates from high school. We know when we experience this feeling that we have shared a little of ourselves. So, why is it that some of us seem to lose this desire?

Could it be that we become tainted by society's rules, being trained to believe life is a series of rituals decided by survival of the fittest? Perhaps it's time we turn our attention toward a more gallant quest, one in which a portion of our energy is focused in an outward direction.

This can be done with the simplest of actions and it begins with the single step of becoming aware. Many people feel they need to be rich, powerful or famous before they can reach out and make a difference, but there are countless food banks, orphaned children and shelters that would tell you differently.

Every one of us can make a contribution to the world we live in, even if it's a simple act of taking in a newspaper from the neighbor's lawn when he is away on vacation.

As soon as we recognize that we may be of service, then perhaps we may become of service. Take one step—do what feels best to you and the reward may be found in the satisfaction of knowing how truly important you are to someone else.

Gregory Scott Reid

IMPROVING ONE LIFE AT A TIME
Steve Mass

I was driving home from a date at 2 a.m. on the 91 Freeway when another car cut me off. I swerved and hit the center divider. At that point, my car was out of control and sped back and forth across all lanes of the freeway until it finally came to a stop. The airbags deployed and smoke came out of the engine. I was afraid my car was on fire, so without hesitation, I quickly got out of it. As I exited my car, I looked up and saw another car coming right at me. I started running in the opposite direction, but within seconds, I was hit by the car and thrown to the ground. Fortunately for me, the car just grazed my heel and I was uninjured.

That afternoon, I returned to my car to survey the damage and retrieve my possessions. As I approached my car, I heard two men talking about my accident. I overheard one of the men say, "There is no way that the person in this car survived the accident." Hearing what he said, I replied, "I am standing right behind you." They were both shocked. I could have died that day.

There was a reason I did not die that day. Was it because my dad, who passed away a few years back, was looking over me? Was it some higher being protecting me? Was it simply not yet my time to leave this world? I have often pondered these questions and I would like to think it was all three.

I personally believe things happen for a reason. So, what was the purpose of this accident? I decided there must be something else I need to do before leaving this earth. Being fortunate enough to survive, I decided that day that I would do things for others to help them improve their own lives.

The best way to help people is to teach them how to do something for themselves instead of doing it for them. One area of daily life that was of special interest to me was credit. This became very apparent when I went to buy a new car. When the dealership ran my credit, they were amazed at how good it was. They were accustomed to seeing people who had poor credit and financing challenges. I realized then that my credit score affected so many aspects of my life (not just when applying for a credit card) and it definitely affected other people too. What better way to improve a person's life than to help him understand the rules of credit? My father always told me that it is better to have good credit and no money than to have plenty of money and bad credit. This always stuck with me. Now my work is all about improving people's credit.

My quest began when I changed careers to begin working for a mortgage broker who hired me specifically to run his credit division. He wanted to conduct seminars to help clients improve their credit scores so they could get into a home with a good mortgage interest rate. I began learning about the industry and we arranged our first seminar to educate our clients on credit. Four people attended the first seminar. At first, I was disappointed at the low turnout, but then I noticed that all four of them appeared to be overwhelmed and having trouble breathing before the seminar started. As the seminar proceeded, it was obvious that they all began to breathe a little easier. By the time the seminar ended, they were all in great moods and were breathing sighs of relief. They were able to see a new possibility for themselves. We had made a difference in the lives of four people in one day. Being able to help those four people breathe easier was a turning point for me. This was how I was going to achieve my goal of improving one life at a time. I had to learn the system and master it to make this dream come true.

In my research, I learned that according to the three credit bureaus, 50 percent of Americans have a credit score less than 692 and 80 percent of Americans have an error on their credit reports that they do not even know about. In this day and age, credit is king, especially in this credit crisis we are having in America now.

We, as Americans, are judged by our credit scores, but do not know the rules of the credit game. Imagine being judged because you do not know how to play a certain game, like croquet, for example. Not all Americans know how to play croquet. Would that be fair? Everything we do involves credit. When you rent an apartment, get a credit card, open a bank account, get a cell phone, apply for a job, get cable or Internet for the house, buy a car or house, you are evaluated based on your credit score. My goal is to make these life events easier for all Americans. Everyone should be able to breathe easier knowing that they have control over their credit score.

Steve Mass

MEANT TO BE
Karolen C. Bowman, M.D.

I believe each of us has a purpose—to improve the world—though not all of us honor that mission. On our best days, we choose to uphold what we know in our souls: that we are put here to serve.

I feel especially blessed to be here. You see, my parents were having trouble conceiving in the early 1950s. My dad had served as a medic in World War II, living the life shown in *Saving Private Ryan*, while my mom furthered her education as a teacher. Both had many relatives, so it never occurred to them they might not one day have the large farm family they wanted—until it didn't happen.

Aunt Ruth was an obstetrical nurse in Charlotte, N.C., and she knew of an obstetrician who was practicing cutting-edge treatments. At the time my parents scraped together every dollar they could in order to afford help. I was conceived in this doctor's office when my father's sperm was injected into my mother's womb. The year was 1952. I was born nine months later. I was unaware of this until I graduated medical school in 1977. Things of that nature were too hush-hush at the time.

I felt valued from the very beginning, although I was never sheltered or coddled and my folks went out of their way not to spoil me. They taught me at a young age to help out, share and give back. They taught by example.

By age 10, I knew I wanted to be a pediatrician. I had learned a lot about childhood illnesses firsthand. I once had a 105-degree fever along with pneumonia and the red measles. I got chicken pox so badly in the middle of one hot summer that the bed clothes had to be wet down so my parents could turn me over without me sticking to the sheets. I was plagued by asthma and allergies and living on a farm didn't help. It certainly gave me experience though.

As a child, I sincerely wanted to help children and families to be happy and healthy. The best advice I received from my rural high school guidance counselor was to go to a co-ed college because I would have to learn to prove myself in a 1970s male-dominated world.

I attended Wake Forest University, a strong liberal arts college located an hour's drive from home. I was ecstatic the day I was accepted to medical school. I believe my interviewers knew I intended to achieve.

Medical school was like dropping off the planet into a wormhole filled with intense learning and dramatic experiences and the acknowledgement that none of us would ever know it all. There were 10 women in my class of 97 students and most of the female mentors at the university were either married without children or single. That was not what I saw for myself; I really wanted a family. (Maybe it was partly because I am an only child and I love kids.) Besides the medical degree, I also became a "Mrs." in the spring of 1977 when I married my true life partner.

Finding residencies in the same area was not easy for a married couple. It was a hard day when we learned we had been turned down everywhere we interviewed with in the southeast. Our chairmen got behind us though and found openings for us at Baylor College of Medicine in Houston, Texas.

We dropped off the planet of North Carolina into a new one that was just as big and different as it could be. We witnessed city problems, rural problems and international problems. We learned to love cabritto grilled over mesquite and enchiladas at a time when Tex-Mex was considered "foreign."

We were constantly soaking up new medical information and becoming more skilled. I focused on general pediatrics, growth and emotional development because I really wanted to be of service in those areas when I returned home. I remember the first day I saw a child with anorexia nervosa—it was a nine-year-old boy, rather than the usual preteen girl. I remember the first child I saw with major attention deficit hyperactivity disorder—a four-year-old boy who was so boisterous and active he could not sit down to eat. I remember my nights on call in the emergency department when there were five patients with bacterial meningitis. Each of these taught a lesson.

I often look back on those years of being needed. My husband and I have been blessed with four wonderful, unique children who have taught us more than we wanted to learn. I sometimes bump into people who remind me of the time I was called in for a bean in a kid's nose, or that late-night call about colic, or the more serious stories that will never be forgotten. My last patient with bacterial meningitis is finishing college this year—vaccines have been dramatically helpful. I see young men and women who once suffered from prematurity and are now blossoming into capable young adults. I see many of my ADHD patients "getting it together," and making career choices that let them shine.

My favorite reminder was when a tall man approached me and said, "Aren't you Dr. Bowman?" He then reached down to give me a hug. I recognized those eyes—they hadn't changed since he was a baby.

My next journey is to grow up with those patients! Many have told me over the years, "I wish you still could be my doctor!" as they have aged out of my practice. After hearing this enough times, I finally called my malpractice carrier and asked if I could get my insurance changed so I could see adults. I now help adults, both young and old, to better understand their health options. I choose to listen, look and teach—in that order. I am still learning and cramming new experiences into my life. I want to go on more mission trips, I want to write more and I want to paint someday. I am proving to my "kids" of all ages that we never stop learning and we never stop serving, because that is the reason we exist!

Karolen C. Bowman, M.D.

MY CALLING
Frank Michael

In the summer of 1961, I was not yet born. My parents had not yet met, but that's when my story began. On August 13 of that year, construction of the Berlin Wall began. It represented a dramatic physical representation of the Iron Curtain, the Cold War and the seemingly insurmountable barriers to freedom, oneness and unification. The split of Berlin, Germany, into East and West can also be seen in the context of the duality of human awareness: the separation of reason and logic within the realm of consciousness itself.

The summer of 1969 represents one of the most climactic and revolutionary periods of modern history. This was the era of free love and freedom of expression in all forms, unbridled by social norms and restrictive traditional values. The unstoppable creativity and musical genius of Jimi Hendrix and the explosion of counterculture and artistic freedom could not be held back. This was also manifest in the ultimate technological and scientific achievements of men of that era. That summer, on July 20, Neil Armstrong became the first man to walk on the moon. It was the culmination of the Apollo 11 mission and man's first glimpse of earth from another celestial body. This led to a transformation of human awareness and a sense of oneness that engulfed all nations and races. Five days later, my parents were married.

I was born a few years later, in 1971, into a world struggling with the Vietnam War, the closing of the gold window by Nixon and the energy crisis. While growing up during this period, I had no idea of the significance of the current world events, but somehow there arose in me a deep spiritual awakening at that early age. At about age 5, when asked what I wanted to be when I grew up, I told my parents and grandparents I wanted to become a priest. I recall reading the Bible and being drawn to the book of Revelation in particular, and for some unknown reason I felt significant changes were upon us and somehow I was called to service.

In September 1989, protests broke out all over East Germany. I had just turned 18 and my coming-of-age coincided with the fall of the Berlin Wall shortly thereafter on November 9, 1989. I vividly remember the jubilation, celebration and the feeling of a wondrous freedom, a new chapter of humanity opening up before me. The sense of oneness and connectedness and the expansion of awareness that accompanied it had a significant impact on me.

Fast forward to the summer of 2001. I was recently divorced and feeling lost in the world. I went backpacking in the rain forest of Costa Rica, searching for meaning in an effort to understand myself. I returned home only to find myself in a deep depression, feeling alone and spiritually lost. Shortly after returning, I watched in disbelief as the Twin Towers came down. I watched the news as shock and awe rained down on Baghdad. An awareness began to emerge in me that I was blessed and cursed by being born during interesting times. A fundamental shift was taking place.

My spiritual calling was reawakened through meditation and the study of eastern religions and mysticism. I fully embraced this new awareness, but struggled to find an outlet that fit into the context of the mundane, day-to-day world of material existence.

I recall being on a business trip in Montreal and coming across a large segment of the Berlin Wall on display that was covered in graffiti. After the fall of the wall, it was dismantled and sections were scattered all over the world to represent the end of the Cold War and a new age of possibility and peace. The beauty and artistic expression I saw there symbolized the path of evolutionary enlightenment of which we were all taking part. This creative expression was a manifestation of the divine spirit that set in motion the creation of the universe. As he watched the Earth rise from the surface of the moon, Buzz Aldrin came to realize "we are all made of stars." This oneness and connectedness with everything was undeniable for him at that moment and represented my expanding awareness.

I realized my calling was to use my creative expression to highlight our common spiritual connection and our shared evolution of awareness and enlightenment. From the creation of the stars to matter becoming aware of itself, my art and creative expression would be my service to humanity in making this realization apparent to those I could reach.

I took close-up photographs of segments of the graffiti that stood out in color and composition. I wanted to capture the spirit of what the original and anonymous artists had begun and transform it into something that included, but transcended, what had come before. This represented for me the constant evolution of consciousness and awareness. The pieces came to be included in a series titled "Path of Enlightenment" and "Levels of Consciousness."

"Path of Enlightenment" includes the notion of Samsara, which represents our attachment to the material world; Satori, which represents the moment of awakening or expanded awareness that comes in a flash of self-realization, and one-taste, which represents the transcendence of duality and complete oneness with self and all that arises from moment to moment. The series "Levels of Consciousness" represents the levels of our being that become apparent after careful introspection and contemplation. We begin with our physical bodies and the molecules that make it up called Annamaya kosha. Our bodies are animated with the life force that permeates and is fueled by breathing out—or prana—which is referred to as Pranamaya kosha. The next level is our mind, thoughts or intellect, known as Manomaya kosha. Upon further contemplation and meditation, we come to realize we are not our thoughts, our emotions or our sensations. We are something that comes before that which is our soul, or the level called Vinjanamaya kosha. Beyond these comes a transcendence of all levels and a complete realization of oneness called Annandamaya kosha.

My creative expression has allowed me to integrate the spiritual awakening and call to service that I felt at an early age. My art and the concepts it represents are part of the common path we all travel as part of the human race and the larger Kosmos (the physical cosmos and all of consciousness). For me, the transcendence of the material world does not mean we forsake it. In fact, we embrace it fully and completely, knowing it is the physical manifestation of the divine realm.

Frank Michael

Go Within
Alison Dunn

To live the life you love sounds easy enough. However, for the majority of us, it's just not that simple. We struggle with fear, lack of money, having little confidence and conditioned thoughts that hold us back from our potential.

For me, this was especially difficult because I had no confidence in my abilities. I felt I wasn't qualified to do or be anything other than average, but at the same time, I deeply yearned for something greater.

My life was as "normal" as any other person's. I had a good job and I had good friends. On the surface, my life looked fine. Yet, in reality, I was nearly 40, single, broke and miserable. What had happened to my life? How did I let it become this empty nothingness? Every relationship I ever had always ended and whenever I was promoted at work, I quit. I could not save any money, so I still didn't have anything to show.

I struggled with inadequacy my entire life. I had very little self-esteem and could never finish anything I started for fear of failure. One day, I was sitting at home alone feeling sorry for myself because another relationship had ended, when I just couldn't take my misery any longer. I was sick to death of it and feeling inadequate, feeling lonely, feeling like a victim and feeling like everyone else's lives were moving on while I sat stationary and lost. It was like I couldn't stand to be in my own skin any longer. I found myself at a point where I either had to end it all or get up off the couch and say, "I can't take this any more!"

So, I got up off the couch, moved out of my old boyfriend's house, enrolled in a university and did everything I possibly could to change my circumstances. It was as though I had become so depressed that something inside of me finally clicked, driving me toward self-development.

I absorbed every self-help book I could get my hands on and decided I would spend every waking moment on self-improvement. At first, this quest was about understanding how my feelings of inadequacy had held me back from material things. Where was my fancy car, big house with the pool, holidays in Europe each year and rich husband?

However, after the months upon months of reading books and applying their concepts, I was exhausted. I felt like I was chasing something outside of me, which added to my inadequacy. Years went by and I still had no fancy car, no big house with a pool, no holidays to Europe and definitely no rich husband. I was telling myself I was looking inward, but, in reality, I was still running around in circles chasing money and material things. I had just labeled it as "self-development."

I was so exhausted that I decided to stop my quest for awhile. I needed respite from my mission. Something strange began to happen. Because I had stopped to take notice of my surroundings and slowed down, I was less driven and I relaxed for the first time in years. I began to notice that everywhere I turned I saw the same message screaming the word "meditation."

It was everywhere I looked. I had learned enough from reading to take this as a sign, so I decided to stop searching for outside intervention and material possessions and just rest for a while to try some meditation. If nothing else, I would be rested for my next onslaught of personal development. Through my fumbled attempts at meditation over the next few months, I made a life-changing discovery. If I really thought about it and if I was completely honest with myself, all I really wanted was some peace in my heart. It really wasn't about the material things at all. I was so tired that all I wanted was stillness, quietness and calmness in my life. I realized that change doesn't come from the outside; it comes from the inside.

In the course of finding a peaceful, comforting place to go every day, ironically, I have accomplished considerably more than when I ran around in circles. It has been a fulfilling journey and I want to give hope and encouragement to those who feel an underlying unhappiness and yearning for something bigger and better. Something "clicked" in me and I have been driven and passionate ever since.

My life now is much happier. I graduated on the honor roll as valedictorian of my class. I have since started my own business that empowers others to better themselves through personal development. I hold meetings where women gather, network and discuss personal development themes. I am also a public speaker, something I previously didn't have the confidence to do. None of this would have been possible before I took my journey inward to discover the real me, the powerful me and the confident me. The old me would have felt unworthy, not good enough and too uneducated to speak in front of people. Meditation and stillness have given me a wonderful feeling of relief, ease and love, as well as a place of extreme comfort. It has expanded my awareness to accept the universe as a blissful place where there is no failure, only love. Everything feels effortless and joyful.

My hope is that, while reading my story, you find comfort and strength in the fact that a young woman with no confidence or skill, who was depressed and felt unworthy, is now on top of the world. I found the courage to start a business, something I would never have even considered before. I now empower others to search within themselves to do the same and I am doing this with confidence and without fear. I say to you that if I can rise above my insecurities, so can you.

If you are reading this, then it means you are already on your way to finding true happiness. You are clearly searching for a happier life, a better life. Stop running. Go inside yourself and find the peace and comfort that reside in each and every one of us. You will find great inspiration and love there. Do a service for yourself. All you need to do is to stop and let it re-appear within you. It has always been there and always will be.

Alison Dunn

FREEDOM
Dr. Michael Beckwith

I free myself from the need to judge any person, nation or event. My consciousness is at peace, for it is now rooted and grounded in the Spirit. My thinking is premised on Infinite Mind, and I am established in love, compassion and forgiveness.

From the center of my heart, I radiate compassion to all beings, knowing that their pain is bathed in the Infinite Love of the Spirit.

I awaken the spirit of forgiveness within me. Even now it fills my consciousness with loving kindness toward myself with all beings. I judge not, lest I be judged. I love with the unconditional love of God.

Right here, right now, Divine Love loves through me. Divine Right Action frees me from the errors of human judgment and causes me to know that all beings are emanations of the One Life.

The true spiritual essence is all I know of each person. I think rightly, and I love greatly. I live to let love express itself through me.

I accept the fullness of life and am a distribution center of compassion, forgiveness, and love. I am blessed and prospered by Divine Love as it flows through me now.

I declare my faith in God and release material patterns of behavior. I know that God is at the center of life and I depend upon that which projected all creation as its own to be the source of eternal safety and security for all beings.

Dr. Michael Beckwith

INSPIRED LIFE
Dr. Richard Tapper

In order to receive, you must learn to give. We have all heard that old adage many times, but the question is, how do we apply it to our lives? There are many ways to be of service to others, from being a gas attendant, a waiter or a janitor, to giving money to a homeless person on the street. We all have the ability to be of service to others every day. No type of service is greater than that from the heart. The service we give to others must come from the heart with nothing expected in return. This is true service and, at a higher level, it is real, unconditional love.

The unconditional love my parents gave me became my inspiration for service. No matter how little money we had, no matter what it took, they always provided me with the best example of service without expectations. For example, my mother was disabled from the time she was born. Her disability had the potential to be crippling throughout her life, but she took that disability and turned it into an ability to serve. She served her kids, her family, her friends and her community by showing unconditional love to everyone she met. In turn, when someone refers to her, a smile always comes to his or her face. To me, bringing out positive emotion in people is the greatest type of service one can give to another. Each of us has the ability to do that.

We all have something inside of us that elicits such passion and truly gives us our greatest ability to serve. In order to find what our purpose is, we must go inside our true selves. Through daily meditation and visualization, we have the ability to figure out what that is. Think about what makes you the happiest—what gives you the most inspiration—and bring that out and share it with others. When I became a chiropractor, I knew the body could heal on its own without drugs and surgery, but it took an experience of service to show me that it was true. As my practice was being built, I offered free chiropractic care to the homeless.

Armed with my hands, a table and a closet in a homeless shelter, I went to work. What started as one patient eventually turned into hundreds a week. One man who I adjusted regularly told me to meet him the next day in the makeshift office at noon, saying it was a life or death situation. The next day, he came into the office carrying a lady in a blanket. He laid her on the table and said, "This is my wife. She was dying in the hospital. There is nothing they can do. Please help her."

I was scared, but as I went inside myself, a calm came over me and an inner voice said, "You can help her, you can help her." I put my hands on her, felt her spine, adjusted her, and suddenly her eyes opened up and she uttered the words, "Thank you."

At that moment, we all started crying and I knew I had found my calling. You never remember the money, the cars, the houses or the clothes. What sticks with you are the moments, particularly the ones that change the lives of others. When you leave this world, these moments are what other people remember about you. Each and every one of us has the ability to change the world for good, but in order to do that, we must serve others. We do it by listening to that little inspirational voice inside that tells us how to live and reach our full potential.

In order to truly serve, you must live in the present. Most of us live in past guilt of what has happened or future fear of what catastrophes might occur. When we live in these states of emotion, we can never truly serve because we are never present in the moment. To live in the present, we must realize everything in the universe is completely balanced. There are equal numbers of positive and negative things out there. This is important because, when you look at the universe in terms of physics, an equal number of positive and negative charges create a neutral charge. A neutral charge is light. In many books, light is considered to be love. In the first book of the Bible God says, "Let there be light" (Genesis 1:3) meaning, let there be balance and love. When you start loving people for who they are, they truly become the people you want to love.

No one can ever take away your ability to serve others. Throughout my life, I've realized the more I selflessly serve, the more I receive. Start by writing down three ways you can serve humanity each and every day. When the day is done, journal about how that felt. These feelings will give you the fuel to be the best you can be. When you are having a bad day, read the journal because it will always bring you back to a place of presence and love. Many of us have the ability to be great in life. When you look throughout history, the greatest people were the ones who gave the greatest service. Jesus washed feet, Moses herded sheep, Mother Teresa helped the poor, Martin Luther King Jr. stood up to oppression. When people hear these names, they generally respond with positive thoughts and feelings. For these individuals, a fire was lit inside them, not to be great, but to serve and keep serving until the last ounce of life was squeezed out of them. At the end of your life, you must ask yourself if you did everything you could with everything you were given. If you did, then your name may just appear next on the list.

Dr. Richard Tapper

SPEAK THE SPEECH, I PRAY YOU...
Becky West

Have you heard the latest? I'm talking about the truth of awesome communication and the effect it has on your life, not only at work or home with your family and friends, but with yourself. With awesome communication, your whole world opens up.

In three months, I discovered I had a voice. When I live the life of freedom I am born into, I create the life of freedom I live, embrace my freedom and offer freedom to others by honoring who I am.

My story demonstrates how anyone can begin to create personal freedom by using their voice. In all honesty, I realize my whole life is a journey and when I say in three months I discovered I had a voice, I'm talking about a specific awareness I gained in that time.

Now, everything I've discovered in my life up to this point has been building, one experience on top of another. In fact, what I share with you are my experiences from infancy, childhood, teenage years, early career, first marriage, motherhood, later career and single parenting. All I have experienced has shaped my being.

The basis of my story is to share with you how I discovered there's more to me than I ever dreamed possible. I didn't know how to communicate. That's right: I didn't know how to speak, carry on a conversation or share my feelings in a way that was comfortable for me.

Physically, I was able to speak. It was how I felt inside that made me feel I could not. Speaking was outside my comfort zone. I looked at it as something I had to do, not something I wanted to do. I didn't want to feel this way, but it was my reality—or so I thought.

My feelings affected my communication skills. My beliefs affected my communication skills. I didn't know it was acceptable to feel angry or hurt, to notice the feelings, voice them, and then move through them. I didn't know it was permissible to express exactly what I felt all the time. I didn't realize I'd be honoring myself if I gave voice to what I felt inside.

The brutal reality of this awareness is that I made this decision as a child. There were times as a little girl that my voice wasn't heard. I was stubborn and practiced not using my voice through my childhood, teen years, my 20s, 30s and into my 40s. The extent to which I used my voice varied over time and circumstance.

I did this so well for so long, I remember being afraid to speak and to hear my own voice. This was my life. It was sadness, silent sadness. It was frustration. I was watching life from the sidelines. It was living life, but not playing the game of life. It was a constant feeling of defeat, of inner drama, of heaviness and heartache.

I excelled at being unhappy. I excelled at predicting what might happen if I tried anything different. I would predict I would be safer if I did nothing—if I said nothing. I excelled at hiding the most important pieces of myself from myself. I was excellent at telling myself I was being the best I could be, without allowing myself to really try.

I excelled at being stubborn about decisions I'd made, whether they were good for me or not. It frightens and amazes me that I had been allowing my life as a woman to be a reflection of what I had decided as a child. Because I excelled in these areas, I became an expert in the field of communication gaps.

My life began to change in the fall of 1994. It changed even more dramatically in the fall of 2007. This was the length of the well-traveled road to improving skills and knowledge. It was full of challenges, signs (mentors, books, courses, audios and seminars) and lessons bringing me to where I am today.

I have a beautiful new relationship with myself and, like many relationships, it grows sweeter with time. I've learned to love who I am. The bonus is, in having greater love for me, I can offer greater love to my children, family and friends. I'm able to receive greater love.

The best and most straight-forward way to tell you how I'm doing now is to say I've discovered my purpose. Does this make sense to you? Do you see an association, however big or small and is it becoming crystal clear that awesome communication is your birthright, too?

I was running from what makes me happy in life. The lesson is that it's not hard to go the extra mile when I'm moving forward in awesome communication. It is in this way that I am able to serve others, by helping them learn to communicate.

I couldn't have done it without my heroes. I dedicate this story in heartfelt appreciation of everyone who has helped me on my road to success. In honoring who I am in spirit, I am embracing my personal freedom.

There is an immediate reflection of who I am on the inside reflected out to the world around me; this is my mirror. In honoring my personal freedom, I have created a beautiful relationship with myself. It's so amazing, so tender and so beautiful.

I truly do see my beauty for the first time. I hear it loud and clear! Now that I am building trust, I'm beginning to depend on myself for all the right reasons. It's only now I can begin to see the same beauty outside of myself. I can begin to hear it! From the bottom of my heart, to the top of the sky, I say, "Thank you!"

I learned success is different for everyone. For me, it's finding my voice, using my voice and helping others do the same. It's setting an example of personal freedom and expression. It's more love for myself and others. It's attracting what I want. It's dreaming my dreams and bringing them to reality.

Dear fellow speaker—yes, you are a "speaker"—can I ask a favor? If this makes sense to you, please put yourself in my shoes. Doing so might give you insight into one or more places in your life where you wish you were stronger in voice. Discover with me awesome communication; speak and be free.

Becky West

How I Received the Man of My Dreams
Judith Spencer

I am a strong believer in the Law of Attraction. Because of the power of positive suggestion, I know firsthand thoughts become real.

Born into a tribe of 10 children, I was a middle child. We grew up without many physical things, but my parents invested in a life of happiness and the gift of the spiritual world. They spent the little money they had so we could take classes under the teachings of Dr. Thurman Fleet, a man far beyond his time. These teachings included the laws of the body, mind and soul. He said we will receive what we ask for when we realize the universe is governed by natural, divine laws.

At the age of 17 I was in a serious relationship, but he broke my heart. Recalling the Law of Attraction, I knew in my heart that something big was about to happen. It would become the greatest gift in my life. I wrote exactly what I wanted in a man on a piece of paper. I listed every detail—the color of his eyes and his hair. I visualized this man in every possible way including his likes, his dislikes and his personality. I read my list every night and pictured this man in my mind's eye.

After six months of daily visualization, my girlfriend asked me to take a road trip to visit a friend who was in a major car accident. Without hesitation I went. Upon arriving, his door opened and there stood the man I had visualized for the past six months. There he stood in physical form. He was as kind and gentle as I imagined.

That night, I told my friend I was going to marry him some day and she laughed because I didn't even know him. She did not understand that for the last six months, I had used the power of suggestion. The next morning, I was excited to get to know my soul mate, but he was gone. I asked, "Where did Ken go?" They said he worked second shift and had to head back to Waukesha, Wisconsin. I still walked in faith because we lived in the same city. I did not know how or where I would see him, but I knew we would meet again.

One evening while I was out, I met Ken again. We danced, and we talked, and he invited me for pizza. He asked for my phone number and said he would call. Days went by without a call, but I did not waver. I understood the Law. I knew things happen in God's time, not mine. After a month, the call came and I asked him why he had not called. He said that it was deer hunting season. I had always wanted my man to love the outdoors. After that, we were inseparable. We spent our weekends up north and lay on the grass. We talked about some day owning a piece of property somewhere around that area.

We were married the following year in 1977. Later, I became a loan officer and sent a business mailer to a city about two hours from home. I received a call from a man who needed a loan. He also needed to sell his property in northern Wisconsin. I asked him where the land was located and his answer electrified me: The land was across the road from where Ken and I met—the place we visualized owning. The Law was once again taking hold in our lives.

We will soon celebrate our 32nd wedding anniversary, and I am as in love and as happy as a wife could be. Our life has been a life of dreams. Most of what we have wanted has come to pass. We visualized our first home, but we did one thing wrong. We asked for a home, but what we got was a home with a lot of problems. After that costly lesson, we understood the power of the Law of Attraction.

For example, if you write down all the things you want in a home, go get a picture of the home, get pictures of items and draw them inside the home. Go get paint samples and see yourself living in the home. The more details you visualize, the better. This is the period of time when you cannot have any doubt. You must walk in faith. You should feel the excitement because you are thinking and acting as if it has already happened in your life. This Law will not fail you. It has never failed us. I have taught others all my life about this little secret called the Law of Attraction. Get whatever you want out of life because it's there for the asking—and always be thankful to the Higher Power.

Judith Spencer

A WHOLE NEW SET OF RULES
Andrew Jones

I sit here today enjoying true freedom for the first time in my life. I am free from the toil and never-ending trials that life seems to inflict upon us. I am truly grateful for everything I now behold—be it my life, my family, my health, my joyous existence or my freedom to choose what I want for the first time in the 40 years I have lived on this planet.

All of this happened in a very short period of time and this was only because I was able to see something I had been blind to for a long time—I discovered how success, wealth, health and happiness really come about.

My whole life changed the moment I started thinking and acting differently. It all came so fast that I wondered where it had been all along, but with a simple shift in how I conducted my life, I made everything happen on purpose and was truly astonished as my life began to unfold in a way I could not believe.

As a child, I fell ill and my schooling suffered to such an extent that I became mentally paralyzed and was incapable of absorbing or learning the most basic of academic requirements. I was soon singled out and being bullied became a regular feature of my education.

Although I came from a very close and loving family, no amount of encouragement could cushion me from the hellish experiences I endured as I went through my primary and secondary schooling.

At the age of 15, it had become so bad that I attempted to take my own life—something I am neither proud of nor take lightly. I see so many reports these days of teenagers so lost in the mire of life and so alone that they have resorted to this pitiful and wasteful act.

It wasn't until I was 19 and had spent the first three years of my career being abused by the lowest of suited life forms in London that I was introduced by my father to a series of motivational tapes that reduced me to tears. The first few hypnotic moments with Denis Waitely and Dr. Wayne W. Dyer® were more compelling to me than anything I had ever heard and they literally changed my entire life forever. This was the first of a long series of awakening moments that I wish to share with you.

Suddenly, the frightened little boy inside me who had failed more times than he cared to admit had walked from the shadows into the light and saw that life was never meant to be awful. There was a whole new set of rules that could be followed if one desired.

This set off a chain reaction that had me voraciously pursuing every piece of motivational material I could lay my hands on. It was a fire that raged for another 20 years, until last year when, after never giving up that search to find a life-changing success model, I finally came face-to-face with what I now describe as a *miracle*. Yes, a miracle that I am sad to say, many never get to discover.

There are many myths in life, one being that we are just a small part of a self-regulated system that tells us to go to school, get an education, work hard, get married, have 2.4 children and work long hours so we can have all of the wonderful things in life. Then we can retire comfortably at the age of 65, when we are too old to really enjoy all the things of which we once dreamed.

There is nothing wrong with self-regulation—that's the way life is the world over. But how many people hate their lives and can't stand the jobs they hold? They hate their boss, have bad relationships, have less money than they spend, don't like the way they look and spend their lives dreaming of winning the lottery.

Sound familiar? If it does, you are not alone. This sad and sorry existence dominates the majority of the world to one degree or another. However, what if there were something that could change everything? I don't mean just the way you think and believe, but something that actually reverses all that negativity and starts attracting everything you keep telling yourself is only reserved for a chosen few.

What I want for all who read my story is for them to understand that, no matter your background, education, economic status or family life, nothing and no one can ever take away how and what you think! If only you can understand this and apply it, you will be astounded at how quickly and profoundly your life will change as mine has over the past 12 months. As I mentioned before, it has taken me 20 years of trial and error to discover this miracle and I am grateful I hung in there to share it with you now.

For 23 years, I had been in a job I hated, with people I couldn't care less about, with six figures of debt around my neck. Oddly, what slowly strangled me was not my debt, but my own anger that my life was not as I wanted it. However, the more I searched, the closer I seemed to get to contentment, even though this was not immediately obvious. Each supposed coincidence that followed was showing me the way I needed to go.

In the span of 12 months, I have left a 23-year career, started my own company and written a book and accompanying CD, which will be published by the time you read this. I have also turned my relationship around with my beautiful wife and awoken for the first time to the limitless possibilities that life has to offer. And all of this came with very little effort on my part other than a passionate desire to change. I am fitter than I have ever been and happier and more prosperous than I ever believed possible—all because I now understand how it all works.

If I could change one thing about the place you are right now, I would open your eyes by allowing you to see through a different pair. If I can do this, then I have succeeded in my desire to help others change their lives for the better, no matter their background, creed, race, religion or belief.

If I can peel back the layers of the illusionary world created by government and the commercial and capitalist reality, I will feel like I have taken someone from a mere existence to a fulfilled, joyful, loving, rich and abundant life—one I wish for all who go on to read my book, *Awakenings*. There is great love for you here and my hope is that you will go on to study this material and others like it, making the wonders that have become part of my life a part of yours.

God bless you all.

Andrew Jones

SERVING FINE WINE
Cheryl A. Michaels

Within days of the September 11 tragedy, I realized that I wanted to serve by volunteering somewhere in a way that would benefit children.

That very same day, I received a packet in the mail looking for volunteers. I joined a group of women known as the Olive Crest Auxiliary. Olive Crest is a leader in the treatment and prevention of child abuse, serving at-risk families and children from birth to age 22.

About a year later, I served as procurement chair for their fund-raising auction. Anyone who is familiar with the world of fund-raising knows that procurement chair can be a difficult position to fill. It is a heavy one that carries a lot of responsibility and usually stretches on for many months. Procurement chair equals lost sleep.

Undaunted, I was genuinely determined to help raise as much money as possible for the children that Olive Crest serves. I brainstormed to come up with a new idea that would bring in more dollars at our auction. Unique, fresh fund-raising ideas are somewhat uncommon and I truly believe that I received my service idea through divine inspiration.

Before I share what that idea was, I want you to know as you read that this fund-raising concept and event has now become ubiquitous in the Greater Seattle area. I can only assume it has spread to other cities, as any great fund-raising concept would. Has it jumped across international borders? Perhaps it will if it hasn't already.

Every major local charity and most smaller charities have copied my divinely inspired idea and used it to raise money for their particular cause. I am talking about hundreds of thousands of dollars collectively. I even receive invitations inviting me to the event that I created! It gives me a great sense of accomplishment and fulfillment to know that I have made a lasting contribution that will presumably live on for many years and raise untold amounts of money for worthy people and causes.

So what was that idea? If you have attended a benefit auction, I'm sure there was wine that was being sold to the highest bidder, sometimes way over the true value of the wine, correct? It occurred to me that some of the wine that I had seen at other auctions was rare, unavailable, quite valuable, etc., and likely came from private cellars. I was thinking, "How do you get the wine out of private cellars and collections and up on the auction block?"

Well, what about a "Fine Wine Procurement Party?" What if we threw a party with wine and appetizers and invited guests to come and bring a bottle of wine as a donation that would later be sold at our auction? Of course, some guests would be *mildly* motivated to bring something fabulous in front of their friends. Friendly competition is a beautiful thing when money is being raised.

Well, my idea worked like magic and we procured dozens and dozens of wonderful, rare wines that were later sold at impressive prices with all of the proceeds going to help abused children! Subsequently, many bottles of wine that would still be sitting in cellars and private collections have been sold in order to serve the worthy causes of our community. I just received an invitation a few days ago to attend a wine procurement party to benefit our local children's hospital. Isn't that fantastic?

Our group is now preparing for its fifth annual Wine Procurement Party. Meanwhile, other similar parties are being hosted around the city of Seattle in preparation for the big auction season next spring. At the first party of its kind, one of my fellow volunteers came up to me and asked, "How did you get this idea?" I will always remember and take pride in that moment, never forgetting my reply, "God gave it to me." Because I wanted to serve, I was able to make a difference.

Cheryl A. Michaels

EMPOWERING OTHERS
Brian Tracy

Once you know how to empower, motivate and inspire others, they will want to help you achieve your goals in return. Your ability to enlist the knowledge, energy and resources of others enables you to multiply your ability to leverage yourself in order to accomplish far more than the average person in a far shorter period of time.

To empower means "putting power into," or "bringing out energy and enthusiasm." The first step in empowering others is to refrain from doing anything negative that reduces their energy and enthusiasm for what they are doing. With regard to those who are closest to you, there are several simple things you can do every day to empower others and make them feel good about themselves.

The deepest need each person has is for self-esteem—a sense of importance, value and worth. Everything you do in your interactions with others affects their self-esteem in some way. You already have an excellent frame of reference to determine things you can do to boost the self-esteem and, therefore, the sense of personal power, of those around you. Give them what you'd like for yourself.

Perhaps the simplest way to make another person feel good about himself is through continuous expression of appreciation for everything that person does for you, large or small. Say, "thank you" on every occasion. Thank your spouse for everything he or she does for you. Thank your children for their cooperation and support in everything they do around the house. Thank your friends for the smallest acts of kindnesses. The more you thank other people for doing things for you, the more they will want to do.

Each time you thank another person, you cause that person to like themselves better. You raise the person's self-esteem, improve his or her self-image to feel more important. You make that person feel that what he or she did was valuable and worthwhile. You empower that person.

The second way to raise a person's self-esteem and give him or her a sense of power and energy is by generous use of praise and approval. Psychological tests show that when children are praised by the people they look up to, their energy levels rise, their heart and respiratory rates increase and they feel happier about themselves overall.

The third way to empower others is simply to pay close attention to them when they talk. The majority of people are so busy trying to be heard that they become impatient when others are talking. This should not be you. Remember, the most important single activity you will be involved in is listening intently to the other person when he or she is talking and expressing himself.

The three general rules for empowering others apply to everyone. They are appreciation, approval and attention. Voice your thanks and gratitude to others on every occasion. Praise them for every accomplishment. Pay close attention to them when they talk and interact with you. These three practices will help you master human interaction and will greatly empower those around you.

The most important thing is to be a genuine, positive and cheerful person. You must develop a positive mental attitude. You need to be the kind of person from whom "never is heard a discouraging word." You should be easygoing, genial, patient, tolerant and open minded. You should make people feel comfortable being around you.

Remember, everyone is emotional. Everything a person does, or refrains from doing, is triggered by deep-seated emotions. Your job is to connect with a person's higher, more positive emotions so he or she feels good about you and wants to help you in some way.

For example, whenever you go into a crowded restaurant, get on a busy plane or go up to a busy hotel desk, instead of becoming impatient with the slow rate of service, put yourself in the other person's place, practice the Golden Rule and ask how he or she is doing. Whenever I enter a busy restaurant, I always ask the waiter for his or her name. Then I use the name while observing sympathetically, "You seem to be working hard today." From that moment on, the waiter always gives me special attention. Why? Because I took the time to empathize with his or her situation rather than looking for sympathy for mine.

Try this approach with those at your workplace. Observe their situation and empathize with how hard they are working, how many difficulties they have, how overloaded they are and so forth. It is absolutely amazing how much better people feel about you when you take a special interest in them, rather than just thinking about yourself.

In life, you always have a choice. You can either attempt to do everything yourself or you can get others to help you do some of the work. Our entire economic structure is built on the principle of specialization. Specialization means some people become very good at doing certain tasks while other people become very good at doing others.

For you to achieve your full potential, you must contribute the greatest amount of effort possible. Concentrate all your energies on doing certain specialized tasks in an organized manner so you can earn the amount you desire and move ahead at the rate you wish. In order for you to specialize and do what you are best at, you must delegate and outsource virtually all your other resources.

Some employees feel the duty of delegating tasks does not apply to them. Even when you ask your child to bring you the newspaper, you are delegating. When you go out to lunch rather than making it yourself, you are delegating. When you go to a full-service gas station rather than fill your own tank, again, you are delegating. You are in a process of continuous delegation from the time you get up in the morning until the time you go to sleep at night. The only question is *how* you delegate.

Your ability to delegate effectively requires that you inspire and empower others to help you willingly. This will determine how fast you move ahead. It will also determine how much you earn in your job. It will determine the quality and quantity of your productivity and your ultimate financial success in life. The key to all of this is your ability to empower others.

Brian Tracy

IN SERVICE: SELFLESS OR SELFISH?
David W. Goodall

To the outside world, my Midwestern, middle-income household appeared to be happy and normal. However, the typical meal served at my home was a plate full of guilt. My parents were absorbed with their own unhappiness. They were so self-involved that the fact I could barely read in elementary school went largely unnoticed until high school. It only worsened as the years passed and, by my early teens, I began to look for ways to get out of the house. I swore to myself I would never be like that. Years later I realized I hadn't held myself accountable to my promise. I was married and serving the same meal that was once served to me. My wife was becoming unglued. Fortunately I loved her enough to recognize what I was doing and made some positive changes. I did a lot of soul searching and was able to save my marriage through service.

I was still very selfish when I got out of college and through my first few years of marriage. I thought life owed me something. I helped others, but only on my terms. So, when my wife decided she wanted to join a team that both trained others for a triathlon and helped them raise funds for cancer research, I wasn't exactly supportive. I did not support her desires and told her it was too much money to raise. But for some reason I decided to go with her to the informational meeting. I sat in the back and scowled at the coaches. But as the meeting went on, the triathlon actually started to sound tempting and later I decided to join my wife in training as well as fundraising.

As my body started to become healthier, my mind became more peaceful. I was inspired and learned I had a lot for which I should be grateful. One of the other athletes was undergoing chemotherapy treatments during the training sessions. He would swim, bike or run between his chemo sessions. His wife and two little girls would cheer him on during the practices. I slowly learned my life wasn't so bad. In fact, it was actually pretty good.

My wife and I accomplished our fund-raising and triathlon goals. We had a great time doing it and met some amazing people. I was beginning to learn that serving others for a higher cause resulted in good things happening for me. I wish I could say the triathlon experience taught me all that I needed to know about living a better and peaceful life; but while I was happy and grateful for my health, my career wasn't going in the direction I had hoped it would and I was incredibly angry about it.

I was working as a support engineer at a very well-known networking company making decent money. It was enough to have a comfortable lifestyle, although working in technical support isn't exactly easy. The customers are always angry and it starts to wear on you after a few years. And I didn't exactly get along with most of my managers. Luckily there was a certification I was required to get that guaranteed a pay raise and carried the promise of opening up quite a few doors inside of the company. The certification exam was incredibly difficult and had a very low passing rate. I devoted a full year of my life studying for it, which meant I would stay at work until midnight every night trying to cram in as much knowledge as I possibly could. As a result of my hard work, I was able to pass the exam on the third try. My wife and I were ecstatic. Life was going to get easier and we were excited about the future.

But life at work didn't get easier and doors did not open. Instead, I was told I would have an easier time if I got certified in a second technology. I refused to do that to my wife again and decided I would just keep plugging along at my current job. Now I was even more frustrated and resentful. I was tired of living that way, but didn't know what else to do.

Around the same time my wife came to me with a typical request. She had been keeping track of a dog on an online rescue site and wanted to adopt him. My immediate response was, "Absolutely not." I didn't feel completely stable in my job and we already had two dogs. Why add more stress to the situation? However, I decided to look at the Web site and check out the dog. His name was Bear and he had been an outside dog most of his life. When he was six years old, his family decided they didn't want him anymore and gave him to the rescue society.

No one wanted to adopt him and there were plenty of reasons why he was still in foster care. He wasn't completely house-trained and he chased cats and cars. He was also close to 100 pounds, so it would be tough to restrain him on a leash if he saw a moving vehicle. Something in me said, "Adopt this dog." Thankfully the universe forced me to do its bidding. We went out and adopted him within a week. I decided Bear wasn't a strong enough name, so I renamed him Diesel.

Diesel was about as bullheaded as I was. He was a great dog, but he was an older dog and set in his ways. For the first time in my life I had to readjust my ways to accommodate someone else. I acknowledged I couldn't control him and then I started to realize I couldn't control every situation, either. I discovered this wasn't necessarily a bad thing. I began to have faith in things outside of myself, something I had never done in the past.

I started to apply this newfound faith to my job situation. I knew that I had to change my way of thinking in order to go forward. I was tired of banging on doors that were closed. When I started to seek out those open to me, it worked. I sent in my résumé to a great new company. I was quickly hired and was very happy with the new position. My friend, Ron, also asked me to help him start an all-women's charity bicycle event. The kicker was that we only had three months to put it together. This included getting sponsors, advertising the event, getting riders and finding a suitable route. In the past, I would have quibbled about these details, but instead, I simply had faith and went with it.

The event was an incredible success and is now in its third year. We were able to hand a local cancer center a check for $40,000 and change the lives of hundreds of cancer patients. I discovered I was most happy and calm when I was helping others achieve their goals. Call it karma or whatever you prefer. Once I realized life wasn't all about me, that it's about providing a service to help others, my life started to get a lot better.

I didn't stop there. I started using some of my "controlling" talents in positive ways. I had always been good with money, even when I was 14 with my first paper route. I cleaned up my financial debt and started looking toward creating multiple streams of income. I sold my house and moved my family into a small townhouse while investing the cash I made off of the sale of my home. I purchased eight acres of land and found the perfect set of plans for my dream house. I purchased another townhouse and turned it into a rental property. I rented a $1 million beach house and flew my family in for a week. It even had an elevator so my 85-year-old grandmother could join us.

My paths in service have allowed me to have all of these wonderful experiences. Fund-raising for cancer research, rescuing a dog no one wanted and co-creating a charitable event that helped hundreds of people have rewarded me tenfold because I was serving others. It almost seemed selfish to me, because every time I helped someone or provided a service, I got more out of it than the recipient. Ask yourself, is being in service selfish or selfless? You decide.

David W. Goodall

Semir's Change of Heart—A Golden Opportunity
Dr. Liliana Cerepnalkoski

I met Semir Mehmedovich several years ago. An information technology consultant at a major hospital in Los Angeles, he is a middle-aged intellectual, well-read, well-traveled and is interested in a great variety of topics. He is charming, well-liked by his large circle of friends and is often the life of the party. However, Semir had not felt well for a very long time.

A few weeks after our meeting, Semir attended one of my lectures and scheduled a personal medical intuitive consultation with me. The reading delved into many areas, including his health. It revealed a heart chakra (a major energy center that is part of the energetic anatomy) that I clairvoyantly perceived as "shredded to pieces." Looking deeper into the physical structure of the heart, I saw anatomical and functional problems.

He told me he had been born with a hole—a shunt, a congenital defect—in his heart that gave him great difficulties. Physical exertion gave him palpitations, breathing problems and accelerated his heartbeat to 250 beats per minute. Lately, these symptoms had appeared even during normal, everyday activities. When this happened, he would have to lie down and rest until it passed.

His cardiologists recommended surgery to close the hole and relieve his symptoms. Surgery was scheduled for one month later. Because research indicated that if a person prepared energetically before an operation, the procedure might go more smoothly with fewer complications and accelerated healing, I suggested a couple of preparatory energy sessions, but Semir never attended.

The afternoon I met with Semir, I later met with Dr. Roger Hirsh in Beverly Hills to discuss renting office space from him. We had a fascinating conversation that lasted for hours. Roger was in his early 50s, with knowledge, skills and clinical experience spanning three continents. He asked me about my life, education and experiences, and about what I do as a medical intuitive.

Roger was unfamiliar with the concept of medical intuition, but understood energy medicine through the practice of acupuncture. He said that many times, while working closely on a patient, he spontaneously received intuitive information about the person, even if he was not purposely seeking it.

He asked me about my clientele and what types of problems they had. I told Roger that they came from all walks of life and had a variety of problems. For example, the man I'd seen just before our meeting had a congenital heart defect.

"And what did you do?" Roger asked.

"I told him to come for energetic preparation before the surgery to help the process of recovery," I replied.

"I think you are irresponsible!" Roger exclaimed suddenly, with an elevated tone of voice.

"Why?" I was shocked. As a Virgo, I am both meticulous and conscientious. "What could have I done, take a needle and thread and sewed shut the hole in his heart, on the spot, right then and there?" I asked indignantly.

Roger went silent for a moment, thinking deeply. "I know," he said. "You could have put an energetic plug in the hole."

I was surprised. How had he come up with this idea? It had never crossed my mind, although it seemed completely logical. I remained puzzled by how he had received this sudden, intuitive insight and I became determined to research it.

When I returned home that evening, Roger's words haunted me. As my family slept, I sat in the dark in an armchair in my living room thinking—an energy plug...the hole in Semir's heart...Roger's words.

I invoked Master Jesus, the healer of all healers, for help. I was determined to help, to figure out what could be done. I imagined Semir's physical heart in my lap. Having gone to medical school helped me with this image. I looked at the large blood vessels and the chambers of the heart, red and shiny.

I imagined high-intensity, brilliant, golden light from the Source entering via two beams into the upper chambers, through the large blood vessels, down into the lower chambers, then arching from both sides toward the septum and entering the hole, forming a golden energy plug. I was in awe. All of my cells vibrated with excitement, my attention focused completely. Everything glowed with golden light.

I prayed to Jesus, asking, "How can we make this plug stay in place?" Internally, I heard a male voice of pleasant timbre specify, "Two energy plaques!" Instantly, two round, flat energetic structures made of golden light appeared, gluing themselves on each side of the hole, holding the energy plug in optimal position. It was a perfect fit.

Amazed, I cried to the Master, "Please, let it stay in place like this until he has the surgery done!"

The voice replied, "Why not entertain the possibility that surgery may not be necessary?" My mind apparently had not registered that as a possibility.

I remained in a heightened state of being—of intense awe, awareness and emotion—I had never experienced before. I was filled with a strong inner, grateful knowing that it was done! In the dark, Semir's heart was glowing, golden perfection.

Several weeks later, Dr. Amneris, Semir's wife, announced that he felt better, did not have problems anymore and subsequent medical tests showed the hole no longer existed. When I heard that, my heart pounded with waves of energy as I remembered the Master's voice: *"Surgery may not be necessary."*

After a final consult, a senior cardiologist declared, "These kinds of things don't happen." An operating room was already reserved. They would check Semir's heart on the spot to decide whether surgery was still necessary. Fortunately, this was not open-heart surgery, but an endoscopic procedure. They dutifully probed inside Semir's heart, found no hole and sent him home. The cardiologists were incredulous.

I wondered how I would tell Semir and his wife, both born Muslims, that Jesus had guided the energetic "surgery," but they are intelligent and worldly people, so I proceeded. They were surprised, yet they had sensed something miraculous had happened when Semir suddenly felt better.

Semir has been well ever since and has been active, exercising on his treadmill, hiking and bicycling. He has told his story many times to friends, relatives and to people who attend my lectures. He wants people to know anything is possible and miracles do happen.

What happened to Semir was not only a cure of his physical heart condition, but also a healing on all levels of his being. Observed clairvoyantly, his energy configuration was optimized in general. He feels closer to God, happy and peaceful. He became very interested in learning energy medicine and his ability to move energy has developed. He feels his mission is to awaken people and expand the limits of their reality, introducing them to new paradigms such as energy healing, miracles and transformation.

Semir's healing has inspired and shown me that, although we do not understand everything, nothing is impossible. By grace, other clients have experienced healings, too (physical, mental, emotional, relational, situational and spiritual). I am happy to be in service and to contribute to the emergence of a new paradigm in medicine and in the world, which includes energy as part of the equation.

Semir's case was medically documented before and after the energetic healing event at Cedars-Sinai Medical Center in Los Angeles, California.

Regrettably, Dr. Roger Hirsh passed away in 2006 from a sudden illness. He will be gratefully remembered for teaching me that anything is possible.

Dr. Liliana Cerepnalkoski

THROWING OUT THE TUBE
Ernie Hudson

I graduated from high school, but not the same way or with the same sense of joy and accomplishment that many people share.

My grandmother raised me and I was told to get a high school education, which I did. However, she never said anything about my grades; I graduated with a D average. Then, to make the road to the future even bumpier, I got married at 18. My wife got pregnant right away, and suddenly, one day, it hit me: This was my life. I was working in a factory and I just felt trapped; I had no way out. I thought, "Maybe I'll go to college." But when I tried to get into college, that D average came into play. I couldn't get accepted anywhere.

One night, I just prayed over the whole mess that my life had become. Finally, I drifted off into sleep. I woke up around three in the morning, and I heard a voice saying, "Go downstairs and take the tube out of the TV." You may not believe it, but I did just what I had been told. Of course, when I took the tube out of the TV, my wife thought it was broken. With no TV in the evening, we had to fall back on simple conversation.

For the first time in our married lives, we started to really talk to each other. I found out that my wife was a great reader; she had a deep interest in people and in the world around her, and had the same kind of aspirations that I held in my heart. Well, we just turned our lives around. She was in the ninth grade when we got married; yet she went on to get her Ph.D. I finally got into college at Wayne State, then got a scholarship to Yale, and then I attended the University of Minnesota. On stage or screen, I've been doing what I love to do ever since.

I can never forget that there was one moment when I just *knew* I had to make a change in things. It was a moment of knowing, "I know there's another way, and I'm not seeing it." Sometimes you just have to ask for help. My life has never been—and never will be—the same. I literally woke up.

We watched so much TV those first months we were married; yet I couldn't remember what we watched the night before. Once we started to really communicate with each other, we realized that we both had dreams—a vision of what we wanted to do, and what we wanted to achieve in life. At that moment, we began to climb out of the hole we had gotten ourselves into.

What's your dream? Young people are often told to forget their dreams and prepare for a life of practicality. Acting or any career in theatre, they are told, is impractical. Well, if you really want to act, I say, "Do what you want to do." I talk to people every day who say they want to be an actor, but they only want to be in movies, to be seen on TV, and to be recognized as a celebrity. There is so much more to living a dream.

I discovered acting in college. College is a great place to really understand your craft; to learn what acting is all about. It's not about becoming rich and famous; it's about learning a craft and being able to do it for a lifetime. I've been doing it for 40 years, and that's what it's about. To really live the life you love, and to live it with meaning, you may have to change your priorities and your goals. It's not about all the pretended glamour and celebrity, because those things really don't matter at the end of the day.

I have four sons: My two younger boys are in college and my two older sons have graduated from college. They have gotten their advanced degrees. I am so happy for them because they have laid the foundation for living a good life; a decent life. No matter what your career path, the same warning holds true: If you are looking for the glamour, the fame and the recognition, you are searching for an empty treasure chest. You are on the road to a very dead end.

So I would say you should lay out a strong foundation, because that foundation is what is going to carry you over the years. In spite of a few moments of possible glory, you don't really want to end up like so many friends I have known who are angry and bitter and disappointed because they were unfavorably compared to somebody else or they didn't quite get what they thought they wanted.

Reality is this: find your craft, study, and train. Follow your dream, but never forget: Before you can follow a dream, you have to wake up.

Ernie Hudson

Tear Up Your "Wish" List and Replace It with Your "Must" List!

Brett E. Bacon, Esq.

I know the secret to achieving outrageous success and I am going to share it with you. This is not a theory. I am a self-made millionaire and founder of a national franchise company. I train other entrepreneurs to become millionaires. By discovering and applying the secret I am about to share with you, I was able to wake up and live the life I love.

So here is the secret to achieving outrageous success:

Turn all of your wishes into *musts*!

I did not become a millionaire by thinking, "Maybe I will be a millionaire someday," "I hope I am rich one day" or "I wish I had more money." This kind of wishful thinking gets you nowhere. Instead, I turned the "maybes" into "musts" by telling myself every day that I must become a millionaire. You must absolutely believe that you will do it. You can't kid yourself. Establish clear reasons for your "musts." If you do, your mind will go on automatic pilot, figuring out how to achieve your musts—whatever they are.

For me, becoming a millionaire was a must so I could provide my family with financial security. It would free us from "survival mode" so we could achieve greater fulfillment and help others to achieve success.

So turn your "maybes" into "musts" and enjoy outrageous success! Once you have your "Must List" written down, review it every evening before you go to bed and again when you get up in the morning. It only takes a few minutes, but you will be amazed at how your subconscious mind will find the solutions to make your "musts" come true.

As you begin to roll up your sleeves and make your "Must List" happen, here are some additional secrets to help you get there even faster!

Ignore conventional wisdom!

If you follow the herd, you are going to get slaughtered. Listen to your inner voice to wake up and find the life you love. Don't expect your family, friends, co-workers or society to give you the answers. Ignore "conventional wisdom" and follow your own path to success—no matter how unconventional or impossible it might seem to others.

Become your own coach!

Trust the voice inside you that says, "I must do this!" You are your own best counsel. I spent my whole career advising others as an attorney, but now I advise myself and I have learned to follow my own advice over the advice of others. You can do this, too. It will not happen overnight. It takes practice. At first your inner voice will be soft, but if you really listen to your own voice, it will be your very best source of insight, passion, courage, resilience and confidence. Always trust your "inner coach."

Disregard the conventional advice of friends and family who do not share your vision of success. Always ask yourself this basic question when considering the advice of those around you, "Have they done what they are telling me to do?" If not, seek out someone who has achieved the level of success you want to achieve and ask him how he did it. Ask him to break down the specific steps he followed, then follow those steps yourself.

Get started now!

There is no such thing as the "right time." There is only now, so get to it. Your plan does not have to be perfect because it will change as you go. Stop waiting for every single last detail and get moving.

Set outrageous goals for yourself!
I often ask people what their most outrageous, impossible and unbelievable goal is and they typically look at me with a blank stare. They are

confused because they have never taken the time to set outrageous goals for themselves. This is a tragedy. If you don't expect great things from yourself, neither will anyone else.

I often tell student entrepreneurs in my training classes that if they think they can, they are right. And if they think they can't, they are right about that, too. Have the courage to set outrageous "must" goals for yourself and then experience the total joy of achieving them!

Be a workaholic!

Yes, you've got it right. I am telling you to be a workaholic! There is no way to candy-coat this. If you want to achieve outrageous success, then you will have to work long, hard hours. I know what you are thinking, "But I want balance in life!" So do I. However, I discovered you can't achieve long-term balance without some short-term imbalance. There is simply no substitute for hard work. I achieved my "must" goal to become a self-made millionaire in just five years. It took a tremendous amount of hard work to make it happen in such a short period of time.

Get up fast when you get knocked down!

You are going to run into setbacks and difficulties on the road to achieving outrageous success. There is no way around that. You will often get knocked down when you least expect it. One of the keys to success is your ability to get up off the mat fast. I learned this lesson as a martial artist. If you stay on the mat, things can go from bad to worse in a hurry. So get up fast, learn from your mistakes and press on. Never give up.

Keep raising the bar as you go!

Imagine you are a high jumper in the Olympics and you have just cleared the bar on your best high jump ever! As you turn around to admire your achievement, the officials are already raising the bar for your next jump.

This is what you should do with your "must list." Keep adding future "musts" to it before you achieve your current list of "musts." Otherwise, you are going to end up caught like a deer in the headlights when you achieve your goal and don't know what to do next. I am speaking from experience. When I graduated with my first college degree, I didn't have a new goal to take its place, so I wasted several years without focus. Today, my "must list" is always filled with new, outrageous goals. After all, you were put on this earth to reach your greatest potential and you can only do that by setting higher goals for yourself. Keep raising the bar as you go and you will be thrilled with how high you will go!

Work for yourself!

At some point in your life, make it a "must" to work for yourself. I speak from personal experience. I was an employee until the age of 35 before I struck out on my own to form my first company. In business, there is nothing as thrilling as starting a company from scratch at your kitchen table then building it up to a successful, national company. I want you to experience that thrill as well. Follow the advice of the co-authors of this book, and you will wake up and live the life you love!

Brett E. Bacon, Esq.

THE CATERPILLAR
Susan Elwell

For 28 years, I worked as a pharmaceutical sales representative. I recently retired from this career to live my life's purpose.

In 1992, after working for two very reputable pharmaceutical companies and moving up the corporate ladder with promotions, I entered the biotech world. After one year in biotech, I lost my job because the company was not able to obtain FDA approval for its product. I was on my second shaky marriage and my daughter was in elementary school. We had a large mortgage and my husband was searching for permanent work. It was a stressful and scary time for me, but after about four months of interviewing, a job came along. I was happy to be the breadwinner, but that put even more stress on our marriage. I craved peace and stability, but thought I had to look outside to find it. A husband, a large house and a great salary meant happiness, right? My dad used to call this "chasing the carrot" and, unfortunately, I was nowhere near that carrot.

I moved from Maryland to Virginia and suffered through my second divorce when I accepted a position with another start-up biotech company. In one year, my life's path included a divorce, moving to a new state and taking on a new job with yet another risky biotech company. I was all alone again. I was an anxious wreck and a lot of that was being transferred to my daughter.

The new company had large territories and a lot of pitfalls. Many people from the core group left for greener pastures, but I stayed mostly because I loved who I was working for—a woman as impatient and energetic as I.

Years later, after a lot of turmoil, the company brought a much needed preventive product to the market and my life got better—or so I thought. I prospered financially and my daughter did well in high school. Unfortunately, however, my relationships with men seemed to flounder as I became more financially successful. I began to think perhaps I could have one or the other, but not both. I started to buy things. I still sought happiness, but I couldn't seem to find a how-to manual. Within a year's time, I bought a time-share and some land on which to build a house and went on vacation.

When my daughter was accepted to Virginia Tech, I decided to buy a beach house and move to Virginia Beach. I continued to buy things—like a Jaguar XK8—but true happiness still seemed out of my reach. Then, in 2003, Hurricane Isabel hit Virginia Beach and devastated my newly-renovated beach home. Fallen trees and flooding waters wreaked havoc on my property and I began to realize my attachment to these things was causing me a lot of anxiety.

A truly life-changing moment occurred when I went to Aruba in 2004 with my daughter. She was in graduate school for entomology at that time and we were both interested in anything insect-related. We visited a butterfly farm and when I walked into the room filled with butterflies, I knew I had found my passion. The butterflies had awakened me. When I got home, I did a lot of research and built a butterfly garden. I educated my friends about butterflies and planted lots of caterpillar food. I was consumed with my new hobby. Four years later, I am still building butterfly gardens and helping caterpillars reach the butterfly stage.

In 2005, I sold the million-dollar beach house and moved to a condo. This was major down sizing, but I felt liberated, going one step further and selling the Jag. I was still working for the same biotech company and doing well, but my wonderful manager had retired and new people were brought in. As the company grew, my ability to manage my territory and solve my own problems faltered. Many people in the company pushed for promotions and vied for power. My talent and expertise seemed no longer appreciated and I wanted out.

Much to the surprise of my neighbors, I built a butterfly garden under my deck next to the sand dunes. No one thought the garden would survive the wind, the salt and the sand, but it did. Butterflies and caterpillars of all sorts came to my garden and everyone enjoyed them. Since caterpillars are easy to transport, I donated them to people so they could watch their magical metamorphosis.

In January of 2007, I decided to change my life. I watched the movie *The Secret*, listened to the teachings of Abraham-Hicks and began to meditate each day for an hour. I became very clear about what I wanted for myself, and then I did three things: I wrote it down, I said it and I thought it every day with intense positive feeling and with the firm belief that it would happen. I did this for about three months and the universe delivered. My clear-cut desire was to retire from my job with enough money to work on what I called my "passion projects." Three months later, the biotech company I worked for was bought out and I was able to retire from my pharmaceutical career and spend all my time and energy on my "passion projects."

Three months later, in December 2007, I finally received tax-exempt status for my biggest "passion project," my newly-created Beach Butterflies Foundation. My goal with this foundation is to build an indoor butterfly sanctuary in Virginia Beach, similar to the one I visited in Aruba, for people to visit year-round. For humans, the sanctuary will be a beautiful awakening place filled with butterflies. For butterflies, it will be a sanctuary where humans are educated about dwindling habitats and toxic pesticides. I believe both humans and butterflies will benefit tremendously from this interaction.

My other, smaller "passion project" is a story I have been writing about a little girl who discovers a monarch caterpillar on a milkweed plant and how she helps it become an adult butterfly. There is a lot to learn about metamorphosis and Mother Nature, and I wrote this story in a scientific, but entertaining, way. My first "God wink" on this project came when I discovered an incredible young artist from Bucaramanga,

Columbia, working in the hotel next door. He loved my story and I loved his sketches of the caterpillars and other characters in my book. I hope to find a publisher soon so I can continue to write about other critters who need our help, such as bees and bats.

I have learned much about caterpillars. Like us, they can transform into something beautiful with a little help. One of my favorite quotes is, "Love is like a butterfly; it goes where it pleases, and it pleases wherever it goes."

Susan Elwell

I BELIEVE, THEREFORE, I KNOW
Nury Abreu, AC.Ht

Our society is governed by rules and regulations that we follow without even thinking. Call it "second nature." These rules are embedded in our conscious and subconscious minds. Some of us follow them to the letter while others will play with them. In either case, they still rule us.

For those of us who do not follow these rules, it is only a matter of time before we pay the consequences of our actions. On the other hand, we are spiritual beings and are ruled by other regulations as well. However, we do not seem to follow these as closely as our human regulations.

It occurred to me that this is why our world seems a little wacky. If we are spiritual beings having human experiences, why wouldn't we follow our spiritual regulations?

As humans, we are either too emotional or too logical. Of course we need both emotion and logic to survive on this planet, but why is everything an extreme? Where is the balance? I feel we need to understand our spirituality and follow our spiritual regulations so we can find the balance in our human existence. We need to understand who we are—spiritual beings having human experiences. Some don't agree.

This book is for those who believe we are spiritual beings. For those of you who don't, I assure you, sooner or later you will, too. There are always crossroads at different times in your life. Depending on which one you choose, it determines how easy or difficult your life will be. This is not about any religion. This is about knowing there is something more out there that is more powerful than anything on a human level. So why not try it and see what happens?

Welcome to my world.

I know exactly when my life changed and when I woke up. Until that moment, I was a jack-of-all-trades and a master of none, full of questions and without answers. I was working as a case worker with the welfare agency when I decided I'd had enough of the rules and regulations. I was in my 20's and I left to become a beach bum. I was the only beach bum with a car, but at least I had a roof over my head. So did everyone else I met from then on.

I had no insurance on the car and it was not registered. My license had also expired, but I was happy.

After six months I saw myself on a flier. My family was looking for me, so I decided to return home to get my license for what I thought I loved most—flying. I thought I needed to be closer to the sun. It was then that my life began to change, but most importantly, *I* began to change.

I was at Penn State taking courses in aviation when my life made another 180-degree turn again. I quit what I thought was my dream. I was in the bedroom and my bags were packed for a trip to my parents' home. I was standing in the middle of that room thinking I really didn't want to go there either, when all of sudden, I found myself kneeling on the floor and putting my life into God's hands. That began the most magical time of my life and it has been that way ever since.

I arrived at my parents' home. That night I couldn't sleep. I got up and began walking around the house. A book caught my eye and I spent the rest of the night reading it. The book was *Three Magic Words* by U.S. Andersen. It looked new, but when I opened the cover I found my mother had written something that made me feel very happy and confused at the same time. At the top of the first page she wrote, "The light of God surrounds me. The love of God, it's all over me. The power of God watches over me. Everywhere I am, God is with me." In the middle of that page she included, "The biggest power in life is to love and serve the people," and at the bottom, "Love God before everything."

The most confusing part was I had never heard my parents speak of God. If it hadn't been for my mother's notes, I wouldn't have believed it. Who knew? Nonetheless, it gave me a lot of joy.

I finished reading the book that night. When I woke up the next morning I felt like a new person. The book answered many of my questions, but not all of them. There are interesting books, CDs, and DVDs that are very helpful for people interested in finding out who they really are. The bottom line is that it is a personal journey you must take alone. People can guide you to the water, but you alone must decide to drink from it. Ever since that moment, my life has been out of my hands. Whoever said we can control our lives was sadly mistaken. From that night to the present, I have been the co-pilot. It's been amazing. Don't get me wrong, I have my bad moments, but I am much wiser now. I know who I really am.

I believe with all my heart and soul that "the biggest power in life is to love and serve the people." Much has changed. I am now serving the people and that higher power with love. I am telling my story. I have a company called Circle of Harmony and I have started a group called The Amazing Gathering. My name is Nury Abreu and I am a clinical hypnotherapist. I believe, therefore, I know.

Nury Abreu, AC.Ht

LIVING TO SERVE, LOVING TO SERVE
Michael Mountain

My 20s started out, as I'm sure those of many others have, focused on friends, good times and partying. I was working on my undergraduate degree, but as to where I was eventually going, I had no clue. What opened my eyes was my karate training. I earned my second-degree black belt, in spite of the fact that I was carousing and drinking four to five nights a week, but something needed to change.

I was 25 when I was asked to teach karate full-time. The mere thought of it terrified me. I instantly recalled a presentation in seventh grade when I froze, burst into tears and ran out of the classroom in embarrassment. However, I felt there was something more for me than just my own improvement in martial arts. I recognized there was a real opportunity for personal growth. I also realized this was an opportunity for me to bury the nightmare of the seventh grade.

With great anxiety and unrelenting nausea, I began teaching. To my surprise, it wasn't so hard. In fact, I was pretty good at it and I loved interacting with students. Instead of enjoying my own improvement, I loved watching and helping others grow and develop, not only in terms of physical health, but in confidence and personality, as well. It was very rewarding. Teaching also prompted me to develop my understanding of muscle physiology, exercise and diet.

I didn't realize I would be using this information later in life, but in my fourth year of teaching, the next phase of my development took place. I had just won the National Karate Championship in my style when I developed debilitating buttock and leg pain. I quickly discovered it was something called sciatica. For six months, I could barely stand, let alone teach my classes. I went to many doctors and a chiropractor and was amazed by how little they knew about my condition. Through my own studies, I finally figured out what the source of the problem was and found a chiropractor who knew how to fix it. At that point, I knew this was my calling. I had a passion for learning all there was to know about lower back problems, sciatica and the nervous system, and I dedicated myself to helping others who had this problem.

Something else happened at that same time. I met the woman who would become my wife. She was energetic, full of life and had a strong sense of self and morality that was all tied up in this beautiful, 105-pound package. Together, we ran off to chiropractic school.

After graduation, I completed a post-doctoral degree in chiropractic neurology, a program that focuses on the study of neurology, neuro-physiology and brain research. This education led to the development of some of the most powerful behavior reconditioning tools ever designed. However, I'm getting ahead of myself, because how I developed those tools is part of the story of my own development. Something happened during chiropractic school, my post-doctoral studies and the early years of my clinic and family life: I developed love handles.

I was 40 to 50 pounds overweight and was occasionally the brunt of my family's fat jokes. As part of my mid-life crisis, I decided to get in shape and not contribute to America's obesity problem. I reviewed all I knew about diets and read all the contemporary books. I picked one that made some sense and went for it.

I fell off the wagon after three short weeks. Frustrated, I blamed the diet and its limitations, so I tried a different one. This one lasted for almost four weeks. I blamed myself this time for failing. Where was the willpower and discipline I had developed as a martial artist in my late 20s?

At this point, I did something quite marvelous—I applied all I knew about brain research to this problem. I realized my food habits and choices were being directed by the behaviors I had developed over the past 10 years. To change my food choices, I needed to change my habits and behaviors, which were controlled by my subconscious mind. On the other hand, willpower involved the conscious mind. The conscious mind uses only two to four percent of your brain, but your subconscious mind uses 96 to 98 percent.

That was it. That was the answer. I had to recondition my subconscious mind to change my behaviors so that my beliefs and behaviors matched my conscious weight loss and health goals. Success would be mine. I developed the tools necessary for behavior reconditioning and lost the weight in less than three months without much effort or frustration.

These days, my wife and I run the Southern California Spine Center, the leading non-surgical spinal decompression and low back rehabilitation clinic in San Diego. We specialize in treating sciatica caused by disc herniations and bulges. I have also developed and perfected our behavior reconditioning tools for both weight loss and chronic pain. We have applied them in our office with absolutely amazing results.

Recently, we made these tools available at Mindsetforhealth.com and we are receiving testimonials of miraculous body transformations from all over the world!

Everything happens for a reason. I chose, in all situations, to find meaning and purpose in all opportunities, whether it was dealing with and overcoming deep fears of public speaking, finding passion and purpose from a debilitating injury, or recognizing the limitations to willpower and delving deeper into the mind to achieve success. The one constant was the absolute love and joy associated with serving and helping others find the willingness to change. Find your passion!

Michael Mountain

What Difference Can I Make?
Vicki Jo Stevens

I clearly remember the cold January day, sitting across the table from Lee Beard. He shared his ideas and the thoughts of Steven E, co-creator of the *Wake Up...Live the Live You Love* book series. It was their desire to give back in a way equal to what they had received.

"Giving is the first sign of real success," he explained. "Chances are, many people have been generous in the creation of an individual's success, so it's only natural to give back."

That's noble, I thought, *but what does it have to do with me?*

That day, the Wake Up Live Foundation began and I was asked to direct its growth. Lee and Steven E seemed to feel that what I lacked in actual foundation experience, I made up for in organizational skills and heart. What a humbling opportunity!

On June 28, 2004, the Wake Up Live Foundation became 501(c)3 compliant and the search for its focus in charitable activities began. With hundreds of thousands of worthy, deserving organizations and opportunities, where does one begin? This was the hardest part. Researching possible charities, organizations and other foundations was heart-wrenching. I began to think my heart too tender to be the director, as I often found myself in tears during the research process. I had to make sure the limited funds were well spent so donors would be assured that the Wake Up Live Foundation was making a humanitarian difference.

It became clear that we could not be effective with a "shotgun approach." We needed to focus our energy with a sure way to track our efforts. In 2006, The Wake Up Live Foundation selected the country of Sierra Leone to be its five-year focus. If you're going to help, start where help is needed most.

As early as 1560, Sierra Leone was identified as a prime market for slave traders and, by the 18th century, slave settlements lined her coast. Soon after the abolition of slavery, Sierra Leone became a British colony, gaining its independence in 1961. In the 30 years that followed, Sierra Leone endured a multitude of coups, the establishment of a one-party state with an unstable economy, horrific poverty and political corruption. In 1991, the civil war began.

If you saw the movie *Blood Diamond*, you are familiar with Sierra Leone and the devastating 10-year civil war. The Liberian-backed forces of the Revolutionary United Front (RUF) abused their power to control Sierra Leone's diamond fields and the money that came with them. Atrocities included enlisting child soldiers, sexual slavery, looting, robbery, rape, mutilation and execution. The Armed Forces Revolutionary Council (AFRC) joined forces with RUF, and in 1999, "Operation No Living Thing" began. The name explains it all.

U.N. peacekeeping troops were sent in, and on January18, 2002, the RUF was disarmed and its leaders captured, bringing an official end to the war. Left in its wake were disease, poverty and massive destruction of the country's infrastructure. Some 75,000 people were killed and two-thirds of the population was displaced.

For the past several years, the U.N. has listed Sierra Leone as the world's "least livable" country. It ranks 177 out of 177 in the Human Development Index for 2007-2008. The index measures not just per capita income, but it also measures indicators such as life expectancy, gender equality, social development, basic educational opportunities and access to public and private resources. One in eight mothers will die in childbirth and one in four children will die before his or her fifth birthday.

It is a sad story that troubles all of us, but I hope you continue to learn more about this inspiring country. I hope you learn how hope, hard work, courage and determination help a country move forward and how the Wake Up Live Foundation is a part of this movement.

The poverty is so severe that virtually everyone in Sierra Leone is continually selling something, whether it be something they've made, collected or grown, in an attempt to simply survive. Although this is a tragedy, they are, at the same time, talented entrepreneurs because of their circumstances. In the same way, Wake Up Live hopes to inspire everyone to become entrepreneurs in their own lives, no matter their situation.

Currently, there are four areas where the foundation is at work. First, the foundation supports the Volunteers in Mission Program (VIM). I'm a "hands on" director and I travel to Sierra Leone as a part of this program. I gather information about the country and its needs and I make connections with other organizations that we feel we can support with confidence. Yearly support for VIM helps provide volunteers who bring medical care and supplies, educational materials, clean water systems, spiritual encouragement and hope. The April 2008 pediatric team treated 478 children and trained 22 midwives and traditional birthing women in lifesaving birthing techniques. A group traveling in January 2009 focused on the continued development of a community farming project.

West Africa Fistula Foundation (WAFF) is one of the important organizations that receives foundation support. There are only nine obstetrician-gynecologists in the entire country. The lack of women's care has resulted in many labor difficulties. WAFF was founded to bring value back to the lives of the women of Sierra Leone by providing them with access to education and resources to help reduce the number of new fistulas and to surgically remedy those that already exist.

Since January 2003, through the efforts of the Africa Surgery Organization (ASO)—a Wake Up Live Foundation-supported group—large numbers of men, boys and even some women have received treatment for disabling hernias. People have had their sight restored through cataract surgery and patients with Pott's disease and scoliosis have been sent to Ghana, the closest place where complex spinal surgeries can be performed. ASO's mission to bring doctors and patients together to provide healing, health and hope to some of Africa's poorest people continues, in part, through Wake Up Live Foundation support.

Sierra Leone is a country with one of the world's most devastating child mortality rates. These deaths are largely because of malnutrition. Project Peanut Butter is a therapeutic feeding program for malnourished children that has proven extremely effective in Malawi and is now being implemented in parts of Sierra Leone. It reports a 96 percent success rate as children grew from near-death into a healthy, nourished condition. This program has great potential for not only Sierra Leone, but for the world. The Wake Up Live Foundation is honored and excited to be a part of this groundbreaking venture. You can search the Internet for "Plumpy'Nut" to learn more about this life-changing food supplement.

The Wake Up Live Foundation has chosen Sierra Leone as its place to be in service. What is your focus? There are so many ways you can be involved in making a difference and the matter of choice can be daunting. Steven E counsels with these words: "When people ask me, 'How can I serve?' I usually say, 'What is your purpose in life? Discover your purpose and then you will see how you can serve others while enriching your own life.'"

You can be in service by giving your personal time to a group. You can donate meeting facilities, furniture and equipment; use your name as a support reference; speak out in support of a cause; or offer contacts for networking and collaboration. You may also provide some expertise such as project evaluation, feasibility studies or fund-raising. And, of course, you can make a financial contribution.

I invite you to support the Wake Up Live Foundation through your good will and thoughts, and, should you choose to help in other ways, I hope you will contact the Foundation. As Jane Goodall, the renowned primatologist, said, "What you do makes a difference and you have to decide what kind of difference you want to make."

Vicki Jo Stevens

LESS IS MORE
Margaret F. Munro

When you hit rock bottom, there is only one place to go, and that is up.

I experienced a pretty traumatic marriage, and a month before our 25th anniversary, I walked out with our six-year-old son, the youngest of our four children, three of whom were old enough to look after themselves. Eight months later, we left the UK and arrived in Sydney, Australia. I had $1, two suitcases and my son, Andrew, who was now seven. I felt as if I had come home. I was scared, but also excited, with a sense of freedom I had never felt before.

In starting a new life, I quickly found that real estate allowed me to earn money and to look after my son. I took several jobs taking care of rental complexes in exchange for accommodations. Three years later, my new partner, Eric, and I took over the management of a large block of units. We managed the letting, collection of rents and general oversight of the buildings and grounds. I also sold the units until I realized the agent we worked for was pocketing thousands of dollars and only giving me $100 each time I completed a sale. What a wake-up call!

Eric looked after Andrew in the evenings, giving me the time and freedom to study and qualify as a real estate agent, auctioneer and strata manager.

We opened our own agency in the inner city and were very successful during the depression of the early 1980s. Other agents were going out of business while we built a very impressive rent roll, which kept us financially stable while the property market was sluggish.

Everything is cyclical, and the market began to pick up. We were on a roll, but I was also beginning to realize that although real estate was good for us, it wasn't what I really wanted. I was discovering spirituality and wanted to delve deeper. We were in that market for eight years and were tired of the rat race. We sold and moved to Mapleton, Queensland.

Have you ever written your dreams, visions and goals and watched them materialize as if the genie in *The Secret* said, "Your wish is my command"? One day, during a quiet spell in the office, I wrote, "I want a three-bedroom house with a big kitchen on 2.5 acres with a creek, somewhere between Maleny and Noosa." Way back in 1975, Eric and I had taken a caravan tour, arriving in Noosaville for a weekend stop. We had a look around the area, and a month later, when we were still there, we had fallen in love with that area of Queensland. We finally left and went back to Sydney. Now, years later, I wrote my goal, and when Eric read it, he said not to be so vague. Mapleton was the place we really liked most of all, so I changed it to Mapleton, put it in a drawer and forgot about it.

We decided to sell and move north, so we looked from the Gold Coast up for a house, but nothing suited us. Then, an agent said there were three properties in Mapleton we might like to look at. To cut a long story short, we saw Lindisfarne, and by 4 p.m., we had bought it. You guessed it. It was a three-bedroom house with a big kitchen on 2.5 acres with a creek. It also had brick on the exposed walls and timber on the sheltered walls, plus a large lounge with a beautiful open fireplace.

There, I created my organic garden and studied massage, reflexology, Reiki, aromatherapy and different religions. I wrote a book of poems and joined so many MLM (Multilevel Marketing) companies people said I was an MLM junky. They were entitled to their opinion, but I knew I was really looking at everything to find the right thing for me.

Soon I found Holistic Pulsing—or maybe it found me. I was at the Body Mind Spirit Festival and kept seeing a stall that always had a line of people. (I don't like lines!) However, I decided something was telling me I needed to join this one. My turn came, and I stretched out on the massage table. The masseur, Michael, put his hands on me and I felt such a surge of energy through my body that the five minutes seemed like an hour. I knew I had to study this.

I joined classes and learned Holistic Pulsing, but as I practiced, my own method changed. It was getting softer and even more gentle. As it did, the results were even better. Less is more.

I gave a very dear friend a brief massage just before she left for a convention in Russia. She promptly e-mailed them to say, "Send this woman an invitation. You need to know what she is doing."

A month later, I too was in Russia, attending the last day of the Free Breathing Convention in Tarasovka. My host had a raging headache, so we pulled two tables together. He stretched out, and I began pulsing him. The next minute, there was a crowd of people around me asking, "What is this therapy?"

That afternoon, we were all in an auditorium and all the foreign guests were asked to come to the front. Then I heard a speaker say, "Margaret will demonstrate her new therapy in Room 504 at 8 p.m." Turning to me, he said, "That's all right isn't it?" "Yes," I replied in a total daze. I had had my first training class on February 22, and this was early June. When you are meant to do something, the universe doesn't mess around. I was dropped in the deep end and I swam.

That evening, about 40 Russians clamored to know what I was doing and how to do it themselves. Three hours later, I had invitations to go to St. Petersburg, Yaraslaval, Rostov, Chechnia and more. "You must come back next year for the convention," they said. I had found my niche. That was in 1991, and I went back seven years in a row, teaching them how to do Holistic Pulsing. I originally called my version "Pulsing for Peace." Through Pulsing for Peace, we can create inner peace. Through inner peace we can create world peace.

Since those early days, my pulsing has become even more gentle and more vibrational and I have changed the name to Vibrational Pulsing, incorporating products I have found through my networks.

Here is a testimony from one of my clients:

"Living a rather hectic business life, stress sometimes takes over and my ability to think clearly evaporates.

I have tried many methods to alleviate this, including the usual medical solutions, only to find they either don't work or have resultant side effects.

After my first pulsing session with you, I felt refreshed and stress-free. There were no side effects—just a feeling of well-being and the ability to think clearly. Now that I have regular sessions of pulsing, my energy levels are higher and my concentration is great.

Thanks, Margaret. I wish I had found pulsing years ago.

Sincerely,

Keith"

In a few weeks, I will be back in Russia to see all my friends there and to give them a refresher course.

Margaret F. Munro

THE ASSIGNMENT
Johanna Courtleigh, M.A., L.P.C.

"We can do no great things, only small things with great love."

—Mother Teresa

We arrive on Earth having already been given an assignment.

Fate or creation or God has set the stage and each of us has a role, a personality, a place and time in the infinite order of things. A genetic lineage, a cultural history, talents, leanings, tastes, deficits, skills. Each one unique. Each, a surprise package. Each, like a magnificent flower. With a hundred thousand delicate details, pre-ordained, etched in, handed down and unfolding as an act of love for life, for the being you are here to become.

I don't know why it works this way. Why I was given me to be, say, and not you, not another. Why I was put into this body, that family, with all the challenges, interests and traits that make me who I am.

All I know is that what was given was grace, and that these aspects are non-negotiable. I cannot argue with them and win! Can't turn this body in for another. Can't wager a replacement personality, though I can be refined. Can't renegotiate the contract, or the fact that I am here to experience and fulfill myself "as this." Here, to accept my assignment and do the best I can to enjoy being me. So that in the end, I leave this planet full, spent, satisfied, well-used. So that how I lived was a way of saying "thank you."

Many of us spend much of our lives arguing with these quirks of fate, imagining if it were otherwise we would somehow be happy, happier. We fine-tooth comb and focus on what we think is wrong. We feed ourselves self-hatred and go to war with reality. We defend misperception and delusion and denigrate the preciousness of ourselves. And we wait...for the right conditions to finally show up so we can begin to truly live. The world is in need of our service and self-love. Right now.

But what is our purpose? How do we serve?

Perhaps, as Mother Teresa wrote, we cannot do "great" things. And perhaps that is not the point. Perhaps service is not something grandiose, something one has to plan and prepare for. But is right in front of us. In our next breath. In how we hold and see and be in the world.

I believe our task is to fall in love with our selves. To live fully as "this one," and enjoy and marvel in the wonder and mystery of being "me."

How do we begin?

We wrap our arms around our pain and begin to speak gently and compassionately to ourselves. We contain and tame and comfort the negative thinking. We practice focusing the mind on what is good, already good enough. We remember to be in awe and not take it all so for granted. We attend to becoming what we wish to see in the world. And most importantly, we step into the now and say "thank you."

And we recognize that we are not alone in the repercussions of what we think and feel and that the energy we generate contributes to the well-being or suffering of the whole.

We have an impact. And that impact matters.

I remember, many years ago, walking on the beach one evening. I was going through huge changes, and it was one of those swirling times when life felt overflowing and overwhelming, and I didn't quite know how I was going to make it through. Even breathing was a challenge. I could hardly find my feet.

And yet I was also surprisingly ecstatic. It seemed that everything in my life was now up for grabs. But I was also filled with an energy, a joy that vibrated every cell: half terror, half thrilling anticipation.

It was one of those wild, radiant nights, with the sun just beginning to set and the sea all psychedelic. The gulls and the pelicans were diving, and an occasional seal head rose out of the deep, looking at me, all sweet wet sleekness.

I came down to the ocean every night to walk, center and talk to God. I came down to where the land met the endless sea, to take my place under that wide, infinite universe of sky. I would dance my body and sing my prayers, and this certain wild, euphoric night I found myself so infused with love, I hardly knew what to do.

And I heard, "Be a beacon."

Send it to the gulls, the dogs chasing, the toddlers with their shovels digging holes to China. Send it to the crazy, infinite immensity of Life. And I realized, we are all beacons, all beaming out our own energy, depending on how we feel about ourselves, the moment we're in, our assignment.

Many of us are efficient at beaming out suffering, misery, anger, resentment, pain. Complaining, criticizing, expert at finding something wrong.

Each of us is a frequency and as we move that energy through, it penetrates and impacts not only every precious, receptive cell of our bodies, but the cells and bodies of everyone we encounter. We affect every cell of the universe with our moods, attitudes and perceptions.

In that moment on the beach, I realized for the first time that I could choose. I could generate delight and joy and become a peaceful vibration of healing and service. Or I could beam out a negativity that contributes to the world's suffering. The choice was mine. And therein lay my "greatness."

The voice in me said, "Be a beacon." So I did. I imagined it flowing out of me, like adoration, like a ray, like an SOS to the amazing beauty of life, my life. It wasn't other-specific. Life was challenging me down to my core, and I was in turmoil, and afraid.

But I was also in love. Perhaps for the very first time.

There is a man who works at the hardware store in my neighborhood. Not such a scintillating job. Not a particularly dazzling man. But every time I go in, I feel his blessing. He asks about my life, expresses interest, looks right at me, smiles and remembers my name. He does this not just with me. (I've watched him!) He goes out of his way with everyone, whether they're there for a drill bit, a can of paint, a sack of potting soil.

Mother Teresa said, "It is not the magnitude of our actions, but the amount of love that is put into them that matters." He loves, walking the world of his daily hardware life as a teacher and minister, sharing this kindness with each one who comes. He will never get his face on the cover of *People*, or win a spot on *Oprah*. But he makes a difference. He serves.

In this way, he is the path. And so is each of us. If we accept our assignments...And claim our power. And recognize that, in our oneness, everything we beam out goes into us as well. We are not separate. We receive what we give. We do it for ourselves first.

This, I believe, is our true service. This, I believe, is who we've been put here to be. We must bring this love. Whether it's being sweet to the guy bagging our groceries, or the barrista pulling our espresso, or the doctor taking our pulse. We always have the opportunity to serve up kindness, warmth, humor, compassion. To make the world a better place, just by how we're living it.

Nothing extravagant. Nothing rich and famous. Perhaps nothing even more important than this. Infusing the everydayness of things. Uplifting the world, one delicate moment at a time. No time to waste…

Mother Teresa said, "I am a little pencil in the hand of a writing God who is sending a love letter to the world."

Let us offer ourselves up to be well-used. Let us write exquisitely and from the heart. For as we do we serve the world and become vehicles for healing and change. We help ensure a future where life can continue, the sea dance its gorgeous flow, as the sky carries us on through its vast, unfathomable mystery.

Johanna Courtleigh, M.A., L.P.C.

Awakening the Human Spirit: Discovering Purpose and Passion in Business
Conscious Entrepreneurs

Within each of us is something unique and powerful. That something we feel at the deepest level of our being is our internal guidance, our soul, our consciousness. It's our passionate vision and mission in life. This intangible force within us is our human spirit. It's that powerful energy that never ceases to unfold, always seeking to break through the walls of our conditioned mind and heart. This life force is present every moment, calling us to be who we truly are and to discover what we really want in life. It is a calling that has led hundreds to cross paths and unite on an inspiring and transformational journey.

An Idea is Born
A brilliant idea was born in the minds of two men. The idea was to combine personal development with income opportunity, the goal being to provide ordinary people with a proven path toward personal and financial freedom. As this idea took root and began to grow, something occurred: Freedom became more of a reality for ordinary people and not just something for the famous. The hearts and minds of thousands of ordinary, freedom-seeking individuals began lifting as the possibility of financial security and personal fulfillment became a reality.

As our internationally thriving company continued to grow, hundreds of conscious entrepreneurs gradually found themselves drawn to one another. They chose to unite in support and camaraderie in order to co-create greater levels of success in their individual undertakings. The Inspired Entrepreneur's Network was born of the desire for human connection and continued business support.

Unity in Community
Being a business owner working from home can be a fun and exciting experience, but it can also be isolating for many. That is why many of

us have opted to unite as a network of entrepreneurs. We all benefit from the human connection and continual growth that comes as a result of sharing our gifts and talents with one another. We engage in collective thinking, personal development and educating others in financial literacy. We have adopted several key success principles which allow us to work with our individual businesses, while staying connected to the greater community.

The heart and soul of our community has grown exponentially over the years as more and more entrepreneurs are drawn to our approach. They tend to resonate with our mission—to help as many people as possible change the quality of their lives for the better. We achieve this primarily through personal development and financial independence.

A Revolutionary Approach

Most would agree that business tends to be a dog-eat-dog world. While most business owners who join us are initially focused on their own self-interests, they quickly begin broadening their considerations to include the interests of the larger community. "But why?" one might ask. Why would a group of independent business owners collaborate when they are in essence competitors? What would make people trust one another, share resources and offer support? How could that happen?

The answer lies in a radical approach to home-based business which has now evolved into a fully systematized international business community. Our Inspired Entrepreneur's Network has embraced the company's business apprenticeship model in combination with a "pay-it-forward" concept, which means that the more people we assist in reaching their personal and financial goals, the more profit we each make. With cutting-edge infrastructure and an extensive support system, every new business owner benefits tremendously from the effort and hard work of those who have come before them and paved the way.

As conscious entrepreneurs, we often donate our time, energy and money to contribute to our larger community simply because we are inspired to do so. Something magical happens when a group of like-minded individuals comes together—each one of us in this community knows exactly what that is. It is our human spirit awakening and breathing once again. As this inspiration moves through each one of us, we reap the benefits of these gifts in our experience.

Given that we have been aided and supported by our network in countless ways, it is our natural desire to give back to the community that has helped co-create our individual and collective potential. It becomes the natural extension of who we are as a result of being a part of this amazing and inspiring community—*that's* what makes it all work so beautifully.

Discovering Purpose and Passion

Our community operates with an understanding of prosperity consciousness and dedication to personal development. Each of us is encouraged to discover our own purpose and deeper reasons for being an entrepreneur. Our purpose becomes the fuel that drives our individual businesses and allows each of us to connect more fully to who we are and what we are called to do in this world.

Through the personal development work and positive atmosphere of our community, many of us have found our own purpose in life and even discovered new passions, talents and gifts. Our thriving community inspires each of us to grow into our true selves. In doing so, we inspire others to do the same. This inspiration continues to grow and expand.

Our community has chosen to have it all: both independence and freedom while enjoying unity in community. We each understand creating wealth is a learned skill which takes a great deal of dedication and persistence, along with a consistent mind-set and an ongoing financial education. We must each take full responsibility for our own success and have a commitment to doing the internal work necessary to create our desired external realities.

We've chosen to collaborate and stay connected to our community because we understand that abundance should be for everyone. We understand we all have a greater purpose in life and together we can inspire one another to discover it. We understand life is more joyful when we are open to learning from one another and when we are open to helping each other grow and expand. We understand the strength of the collective mind is infinitely more powerful than any single person can ever be. We understand business and life are so much more fun when they are shared experiences. Finally, we understand ordinary people are doing extraordinary things each and every day and we are all destined for greatness.

Sharing the journey to freedom with those who can hold our individual and collective vision is what makes the ride that much more enjoyable and meaningful.

Conscious Entrepreneurs

NOT BULLET-PROOF
John Assaraf

I have been blessed: at an early age I learned the value of my health. Plenty of people spend two or three decades believing they are "ten feet tall and bullet-proof," but at the age of 17, I was introduced to the reality in a major car accident.

For several months I had no choices concerning my physical condition. Then I started an intensive rehab program. Up until that point, my dream, like that of many other kids, was to play professional basketball. The dream still lingered when, at 21, I was diagnosed with ulcerative colitis. I was absorbing 25 pills a day, including cortisone enemas to help with the severe pain and discomfort of that disease.

It doesn't sound like the story of someone who is "blessed," does it? Yet, it is true, and the reason is simple. Long before it was too late and long before I could develop poor habits, I was shown beyond any doubt that God only gave me one body to hang around in. My job is to keep it in the best operating condition that I can. That includes both the physical and mental elements of the self.

I made that discovery when I was young enough to understand that my body is breakable. I decided that I would not be unable to enjoy the quality of my life due to the abuse of this miracle called a body. As I got older I also became aware of the spiritual side of my being. I learned how meditation and calmness allow me to be at peace.

So, today, my regimen includes a daily meditation to connect with the source that created me, along with a workout to keep this body in high gear. I play life to the fullest, and I want this vehicle to last as long as it can. My responsibility is to learn as much as I can about the latest and best practices to make this happen. Prioritizing my physical and mental well-being above work and social concerns allows me to take care of me first.

Is that selfish? I think not, for my belief is that everything we do is better if we do our best.

John Assaraf

THE LADDER OF LOVE
Aine Belton

Love radically raises your personal energy and allows life to become the effortless dance it was always meant to be. It opens the door to happiness and joy. Dreams come true and it is the ultimate consciousness raiser and purifier.

Love lies at the heart of all that you seek and separation from it is at the root of your troubles and pain. There is ultimately nothing love cannot heal, transform and transcend.

The Ladder of Love is a five-step process to help you access more love in your life.

Loving yourself or others can be easier at certain times than others. When everything is going great, when you're on a high and life is singing sweet tunes around every bend, loving yourself and others is easy, effortless and natural. Yet, it is when things are not so smooth that you need love the most.

The steps outlined in the Ladder of Love, below, can be used in relation to yourself, another or any situation in which you are experiencing blocks to happiness and success.

For the purposes of the example below, it has been explored in relation to loving yourself.

Foundation

Place your ladder on the foundation of knowing that you are loved. You are loved not only by people in your world, but by the source of creation itself, whatever name you hold for such. You are loved totally and unconditionally. There is nothing you need to do to win that love and nothing you can do to lose it, for you are loved completely.

You are and always will be inherently loveable and loving. Becoming aware of this truth connects you to your true value, increases your sense of worth and deserving, heals the pain of separation and opens you to the love that is there for you in every moment.

The Sides of Your Ladder

The two sides of your ladder are compassion and responsibility. These hold the rungs in place, guide and smooth your journey and keep you from falling off into the traps of blame, judgment, guilt and victimization.

Climbing the Ladder

1. Acceptance

Accept yourself for who and where you are right now. Accept all parts of yourself, especially the less-than-pretty sides, as it is these parts of you that need your love the most. It is impossible to love yourself (or others) without acceptance.

Rather than resist, deny, condemn or judge that which you dislike about yourself, simply acknowledge and accept. As a result, you create the space for release, healing and transformation.

You are not your dark sides, negative self-concepts, failings or mistakes. Your negativity is founded in misunderstandings about yourself and life, faulty perceptions and beliefs about who you truly are and a blindness to your true worth, beauty and magnificence.

When you accept yourself for who you are right now, you will automatically begin to transform; you will change for the better. What you accept you can more easily release in order to become more of who you truly are. Conversely, it is what you resist that persists.

2. Forgiveness

When you have reached a place of acceptance, you can further let go of everything that stands in the way of love through forgiveness.

You are human and you make mistakes. While it is essential to take responsibility for yourself and your life, it is also vital to forgive yourself for any perceived failings or mistakes. With forgiveness, you can return to a place of truth and love. Forgiveness is one of the most powerful forces for healing and transformation and will liberate you from toxic emotions and draining attachments. It is the ultimate mind-body-soul detoxification.

When you forgive yourself, you become more forgiving and compassionate toward others, for you no longer blame them for your projected self-judgments. Some things may seem unforgivable. However, you can forgive the "why" behind a behavior (i.e. the dysfunction or pain at its root that may have caused the behavior) rather than the "what," which is the actual behavior itself. When you take full responsibility for your reality and when you realize it is a hologram of the entirety of your consciousness, all forgiveness can be seen as a self-forgiveness.

3. Appreciation

Once you have forgiven, you move up the ladder to appreciation. Appreciate yourself for your qualities, your strengths, gifts and talents, your desire to love, to give and to grow, your beauty and passion and the love and care you have for yourself and the people in your world.

One way to appreciate yourself more is to look at what you appreciate in others. You will find your own beauty, light and goodness, because you would not appreciate a quality in another unless those very qualities existed within you at some level. The people and qualities that you admire and appreciate can represent your "*light shadow*"—the denied positive aspects of yourself. Own them and appreciate them for being a part of who you are.

4. Gratitude

From appreciation, gratitude begins to flow. It is a natural extension of appreciation and opens you further to what you love about yourself, others and the world, attracting more of those qualities into your life.

Acknowledge all that you feel grateful for in your past and present, from experiences and qualities to people and things. Feel grateful to your future also—who you are becoming and the dreams you are creating. Feel grateful even to those who may have challenged or hurt you in your life, because they will have been catalysts for growth, healing and learning. Feel grateful to the universe for its abiding love and support on every step of your journey. Feel grateful, of course, for your wonderful, magnificent self.

5. Love

When you can feel appreciation and gratitude for yourself and others, the door to love has opened. Allow love to flow into your heart and fill your being. Imagine it as a beautiful light or energy that flows from your heart, saturating you and spilling out into your world to bless, heal and brighten your life and other people's lives.

Let it dissolve and heal any pain or negativity. Let it cleanse and transform you. Bathe in the wonder and beauty of love. There is nothing that will raise your energy faster or more profoundly than love.

Be loving to yourself or another, even if it is just to say, "I love you."

Express your love through giving, respecting, honoring, caring, valuing and understanding. Be open and honest with yourself and others to enable greater intimacy and trust.

Express your love in all that you do—your work, your relationships and the people you meet in your day-to-day life. Let it fill your life with its magic.

When you love, you connect to the highest aspect of your being and shine your light in the world. From this place of light and truth, you can connect to the vision and wisdom of your higher self that will provide you with inspiration and insight. Let love bless and illuminate you and your world.

Aine Belton

How Can You Get There From Here?
Joe Lone

How do we get there when we don't know which path to take? Are we even aware of the path we're on now?

The destination is referred to as often as you bring up the topic, pick up a document or experience the death of a family member or a close friend. Going to another level of understanding is almost as exciting as discovering a new town or what lurks around that next corner.

When I was four years old, I started my first paying job and I immediately had to learn the techniques for success. Before that, I'd had years of job training. First, I had to assure the doctor I'd be a good baby, even if he spanked me instead of hugging me when I came into the world. Then, I had to smile and gurgle on my mother's stomach in warm, loving acceptance of her warmth and love. Subsequently, I had to learn teamwork. If I cried, someone fed me. If I wet my diaper, someone changed it and told me I was cute.

In my fourth year, I inherited a four-house paper delivery route. My brother, Jimmy, promised me a raise if I was a worthy employee.

I studied the skills of knocking first and then presenting the paper to the customer or placing it on the table. The bonus was learning customer relations and my smile spoke volumes. I handed the *Timmins Daily Press* to the Levers, the Pelkys and the Gillespies, ensuring the doors were closed on the way out. Thus, I started a 10-year career and an awesome lesson in spirituality.

I learned to build community, engage in small talk, share news, handle business and move at a quick pace every day. Problem solving, mediation, respect for property and networking were included in my interaction with the fabulous people who lived and worked in my small community.

God provided balance, as the work only took an hour a day, which left plenty of time to play two-man baseball, team football or hockey.

During that time, we went on adventures, biking or hiking to Sucker Creek or to High Rocks at the Preston cyanide dam. We trekked miles of commando trails, playing for hours while admiring the wildlife in their natural habitat.

Leadership was open depending on the activity. When one season finished, another had already begun. Fellowship was always the unwritten rule. The language was simple and "Did you have fun?" was the only question to begin dinnertime sharing. Little did we know how profound and mystical that question was. Our red faces and the earth smeared on our tank pants told everything that needed to be added.

High school was a time to hone our reading, writing and math skills. They followed a close third to another level of community building— bonding through sharing and admiring the coaches who appeared for every activity imaginable. Did we say "thank you" enough for the laughter of our neighbors and for the songwriters who entertained us or to those who gave us a second serving of dinner for our teenage appetites?

Professional life was a challenge of the body, mind and spirit. Could I emulate the great teachers I had encountered in my past? All too soon the awareness that teaching was learning—and vice versa—hit home. Ecstasy and magnificence were involved in the process.

What becomes clearer now is that God spoke volumes as a silent witness through all of my nature experiences. His earth on my jeans, fire in my eyes and wind in my sails allowed His magnificence to grow and grow within me.

Whether meditating by oneself or lecturing to the masses on human rights, we have the opportunity to praise Him every second and to receive His blessings.

The wake-up call comes in different ways, but it always allows us to direct our intentions through Him and to Him. The schools of life are alive with the stories of others who have experienced wonder and awe. The rewards are infinite and are available to each soul, at each moment and in every unique form.

Hear the stories of Jesus and Buddha, then create your own experiences of wonder and awe. In my awakening, I was wide-eyed, watching the person next to me gently levitate. That breathtaking effect lasted until that same experience produced a bolt of lightning out of my elbow. What an immediate, wonderful feeling of love.

I shared with Him.

In my quiet review, I wondered about this newfound relationship and thought about the past. I remembered being 10, dangling 80 feet above a dam. "Please help me!" I was afraid, and how simple was the request.

Christ gripped the rocks using my blue jeans, just as my tired fingers slipped off the ledge.

As we quiet the mind, still in the moment, and all those seemingly unrelated memories and fabulous feelings of love, wonder and exhilaration float by, aren't we just so comforted, knowing we were there all the while?

Heaven on Earth.

Joe Lone

FROM ONE TO A MILLION
João Dias de Oliveira and Cynthia Oliveira

She said her life was over before it even began though she was barely old enough to be considered an adult. She had been abandoned by her mom, a drug addict who did not make enough money to support both of them. I took her in despite the harsh looks from the neighbors and hushed rumors of her past, which were whispered in the streets around our home. She was young and had gone through more in her minimal years than most adults experience in a lifetime. Her name, Michelle, was given by her mother, which was taken from her Grandma's favorite Beatle's song.

Michelle survived the infamous Candelaria killings of July 1993, and I adopted her in September of that same year. She was only eight years old then and one of the many homeless children roaming downtown Rio de Janeiro. One fateful night, she was stranded about a mile away from the shooting site. A rich couple bought her a pizza in one of the restaurants around the American Embassy in Castelo in downtown Rio. She arrived late at the rendezvous place where the kids used to sleep and it saved her life.

Michelle was different from the other kids in many aspects. She was blonde—looking much like a ragged Barbie doll and catching the attention from the passers-by. She always had a smile on her unwashed face, guaranteeing money and food. She lacked the aggressiveness the other homeless kids had and never blamed the world for her predicament. She was liked by the other kids and they treated her as the sister they never had.

After we came home to Miami Beach, the struggle continued. She used to have nightmares about the massacre and did very poorly at school in the beginning, requiring continuous counseling and help.

Years later, we moved to Miami Springs and the Greenway Drive environment helped her. My wife and I took turns walking with her after school, talking about the day's occurrences and planning for the future.

Praying and reading inspirational books also helped bring back confidence in her potential, trust in her fellow man, and above all, knowledge of and a relationship with God. Little by little, she was able to let go of her past traumatic experiences, and it was with great happiness that we saw her light shine through.

On her 18th birthday, I sat her down and handed her a beautiful butterfly charm I had purchased for her and got ready to help her out of her shell. I explained to her that her fear of life would only prevent her from living. Life is what you make it with every decision and every step you take. Though you may take a wrong step here and there, you can always go back and correct your errors, but you can't do this if you never take a step at all.

She needed to understand that she had to break free of the cocoon she had retreated into and enjoy her new butterfly wings to do with this world what she could. Becoming a butterfly is not easy, but how else do you expect to fly? I needed her to know that I didn't care about her past—which she had little control of—but that I cared for her future. She was the only one who could expose her colors to the world she was hiding from, and as hard as it could be, she had the power to make it magnificent. I suggested to her that she should "let go and let God," as we had learned from one of the tapes we used to listen to together. I also reminded her of her divine essence and of the power that lies within all of us. I told her she could undo the mindset that had blocked her from viewing her true nature.

Then I held her hands. We closed our eyes and we prayed to God that she could know her path to happiness. She thanked me and retreated to her room for the rest of the night. The following day, she woke up with a new light in her eyes and a faint blush to her cheeks. The changes from that moment on were almost unbelievable even for me and I am a true believer!

She worked hard in her studies, finishing high school with a full scholarship. She is currently attending a university and will become a very good pediatrician. She says she wants to help children. She says her vacations will be to Rio de Janeiro, helping poor children in the slums. The sparkle in her eyes since that day after her 18th birthday never left.

At the age of 21, she moved out of my house and bought her own little apartment close to the school.

She worked part-time in a pediatric clinic where she would also do her internship when the time came, making more per hour than most other young adults her age. She still visits every week and tells stories of school or patients. It's amazing to see how far she has come from the time I took her in so long ago. It's clear she shattered that empty shell she had used to protect herself.

Michelle told me that with every child she helps, she thinks of me and all the years I fed and sheltered her without asking for anything in return. Even though I had received dirty looks for taking in a girl with a past like hers and cared for her as family, I would do it again. Because, as much as you fear for all the wrong that might come from a decision, you have to keep in mind that if you don't take a risk, you will never see all the good that could come. I helped one girl, and she, in turn, will help millions more.

In the end, a service to a little girl became a service to mankind.

João Dias de Oliveira and Cynthia Oliveira

SEE WHAT YOU WANT
Bill Harris

Until about age 40, I was definitely not living the life I loved. I was chronically angry, often depressed, and had one abysmal relationship after another. I had no real career and no idea how to create one. The direction of my life was down or, at best, sideways.

This was all a blessing in disguise though, because it created an intense motivation to learn what happy, peaceful and successful people did that I wasn't doing.

Today, I'm married to a wonderful woman who really loves me. I make ten times what I used to fantasize about. Plus, I have a challenging career doing something I love.

My anger problem is gone, and I haven't been depressed for even a minute in nearly 15 years.

Now, at age 54, I truly am living the life I love. This transformation happened when I discovered a few key principles that created tremendous positive change for me. They will work for you, too.

What are these secrets?

First, happy people acknowledge that they are creating their reality internally and externally. They see circumstances as an influence, but know that what they do inside creates how they feel and behave and what people and situations they draw to themselves.

For most people, processing external circumstances happens unconsciously. This makes it seem as if circumstances cause your feelings, behavior, and what you attract into your life. When this happens, it seems as if you are the effect of external causes over which you have no control.

Happy people, however, even if they can't see how, know they're creating whatever is happening. They take responsibility.

Another characteristic of happy people is that their actions are the result of the possibilities they see. Where the unhappy person sees a challenge as impossible, the happy person sees what is possible. And, by focusing on what is possible, happy people make those possibilities come true.

A third characteristic of happy, successful people: They focus their minds on what they want and keep their minds off of what they do not want.

Take prosperity, for instance. You could focus on not being poor, or you could focus on being rich. That is, you could make a mental picture of poverty, wanting to avoid it, or you could create a picture of being wealthy, wanting to move toward it.

In both cases, the intention is the same, but your brain doesn't care about your intentions. It just sees the literal content of the picture. When you focus on riches, it thinks you want riches and motivates you to see opportunities, find resources and take action to be rich.

When you focus on not being poor, it sees a picture of being poor and motivates you to see opportunities, find resources and take action...to be poor.

Most people focus on what they want to avoid without realizing the consequences. When they get what they didn't want, they assume they didn't focus hard enough and redouble their efforts. This creates even more of what they don't want, which creates more frustration.

The other penalty for focusing on what you don't want is that you feel bad. In fact, all bad feelings and negative outcomes are the result of focusing on what you do not want. Instead of unconsciously and automatically focusing on what you don't want, consciously and intentionally focus on what you do want. When you do this, you instantly begin to create it, and you instantly feel good.

The final characteristic: Happy people are consciously aware. As a result, their brains are less likely to run on automatic, creating internal states and external outcomes they did not intend and do not want.

First, become more consciously aware through meditation. Though traditional meditation is very beneficial, at Centerpointe Research Institute we use an audio technology called Holosync to create deep, meditative states, literally at the push of a button. This greatly accelerates the meditation process and allows you to create increased conscious awareness very quickly.

Second, investigate your own beliefs, values, ways of filtering information, strategies for decision making, motivations and other internal processes. Centerpointe's Life Principles Integration Process is a structured way of investigating and changing these internal processes, allowing you to take charge of how you create your internal and external results.

There is a price to pay to live the life you love. But paying it is a joyful enterprise that will benefit you for the rest of your life. You create your reality, so learn to focus your mind on what you want, and increase your conscious awareness through meditation and self-inquiry.

The life you love is waiting for you!

Bill Harris

THE LITTLE THINGS CAN MAKE A HUGE DIFFERENCE
Tony Bourke

The word "service" has many definitions; however, the use of service in a positive way will change your life for the better.

I discovered service was high on my list of values at a one-week personal and business growth seminar I attended in the mid 1990s. Once I identified that I had the drive to serve, I was then able to tap into this positive value and start using it to change my life.

Up until that time, I had worked in various jobs and at various companies within the insurance industry. Like any multi-national industry, the definition of service varied depending on the company and the people working for it. I saw many examples of customers and employees being treated in what I thought was an unfair manner through poor and inefficient service. It made me look for a way to help serve customers in a positive way and make a difference to the industry. I needed to find a part of the industry where I could serve customers by always acting in their best interests. It was this that led me to become an insurance broker, someone who has the responsibility of always acting in the best interests of their clients.

After a number of years of working for others, I now work for myself and have learned one extremely valuable lesson regarding service: The service you provide to others is what makes you unique. If you were to ask my customers why they deal with me, they will tell you it is because the service I provide to them is unique when compared to others in my industry. It is because of the service I give them that I can happily say I do not have any competition, even though there are many others who work in my industry. It's all about making your customers feel like they are your only customer in every dealing you have with them.

Serving others in a positive way rewards you by removing you from the stress and worry of the competitive mind and moving you to the peace, happiness and stress-free environment of the creative mind. Serving others you come into contact with in this positive way will mean that as a business person, you will never have to "sell" anyone your product or service ever again. Those who provide good service to all they come into contact with will naturally receive more clients and financial reward through the universal Law of Reciprocity. This law essentially says that in order to get, you must first give. In service terms, you could say in order to be served, you must first serve others.

In addition, it is my experience that by serving others in a positive way, you will find that you will also feel better on physical, mental and spiritual levels.

So who do you need to serve? In my experience, the following categories will cover it for you:

Customers and Clients
Always give your customers and clients more than they expect from you. It could be as simple as sending them a card or a gift to thank them for doing business with you. You could refer them to someone who can help them with another type of service or product they need. Or you could suggest a good book or CD on personal or business development.

Family
We all know that our families are a critical part of our lives and we need to make time every day to provide them with quality time. You should always make sure your day includes time for your partner and children, time in which you are fully present with them in body and mind.

In addition, you need to keep in touch with your extended family, such as your parents and siblings. Never allow things such as petty arguments to simmer until they cause irreparable damage to your family bond.

Friends

It is easy to get caught up with daily life, causing you to neglect to stay in touch or spend time with your friends. You owe it to your friends to remain in contact, as they are the ones who have supported you when you needed it.

Never allow yourself to start saying things such as, "I won't contact them because they never call me," or, "I'm always the one who has to make contact." It does not matter who keeps the contact flowing. The important thing is to maintain contact and maintain your friendships.

Employees, Colleagues and Business Associates

You owe it to your employees, colleagues and business associates to always do what you can to help them achieve more in their lives. These are the people who help your business grow. It is by doing this that you will be rewarded in your business.

Give your employees the opportunity to advance in their careers and their financial futures through incentives. Always be on the lookout for ways you can help other businesses associates advance their business by providing them with referrals or sharing ideas that have worked for you. Serve other colleagues by always doing everything that your job requires you to do. By doing this, you are doing your part to serve the team.

Other Human Beings and Living Things

Serve all other human beings and living creatures in the world by always helping them to have a better day. This can be as simple as just smiling and saying "hello," as you walk past or letting someone merge in front of you in a traffic jam. Just do whatever little thing you can do to make someone else have a better day.

Yourself!

This is the most important person to serve. You owe it to yourself to always take the time you need to keep your life balanced.

Serve yourself by finding time every week for all three areas:
Physical: Regular exercise, good diet
Mental: Books that expand your mind
Spiritual: Meditation, relaxation, community service, etc.

Remember to serve others without thought of the financial reward for yourself. You will find that the more you do to serve the world, the more reward you will receive on every level of your being.

Since discovering the true meaning of service, every day I spend on the planet is a great day and each day brings great rewards for my family and me.

Tony Bourke

SMALL MIRACLES
Nick DeCastro

My wife, Sue, and I were married in 1998 and bought our first home right away. After a year of marriage, we decided it was time to start a family. After six months of trying, my wife was pregnant. It was a joyous occasion! I remember mimicking George Costanza on *Seinfeld* when he thought had gotten his girlfriend pregnant: "I'm a father! My boys can swim!"

Life was good for the DeCastros.

Twenty weeks into the pregnancy, we went to the hospital for the first ultrasound. I was asked to wait outside for the initial part of the test. They would come and get me near the end. I waited, thinking about work and bills—everything but the routine test. However, when the door finally opened, instead of a nurse, I saw my wife rushing toward me in tears.

"What happened?" I asked, in shock.

"I don't know. Something's wrong and they won't tell me."

I almost pulled the door from its hinges as I crossed to the nursing station in a few long, brisk strides. Before I could say anything, the nurse put up both hands and said, "Speak to your doctor. I'm not allowed to say anything."

The doctor was soft spoken with a gentle demeanor. He sat down with us and spoke like a concerned friend. "The baby has a condition called anencephaly, a spinal defect whereby the spinal cord is not attached to the brain during early development. The baby cannot survive outside the womb. We recommend you terminate the pregnancy."

My wife wept uncontrollably; I cursed under my breath. How could this have happened to us?

Though I wasn't religious, Sue and I both grew up in Christian homes. Suddenly, all of the old teachings came flooding back, making this not only a personal tragedy, but also a moral dilemma.

We drove home in silence. After conducting my own research, I realized that the decision to end the pregnancy had already been made for us.

I sat down at the kitchen table, put my head in my hands and wept. Sue held me, both of us crying as much for ourselves as for our baby. Again, I wondered how this could have happened to us.

The day of the D&C procedure, Sue should have been ready to leave the hospital within three hours of the procedure, but instead of bringing my wife out to me when it was over, they wheeled her bed into a hospital room. I went in to see her, finding her eyes closed as she wavered on the edge of consciousness.

The nurses asked me to leave while they examined her. Moments later, one of the nurses sprinted from the room, heading for the nurses station. She paged the surgeon, repeating an emergency code over a loudspeaker. In Sue's room, I watched the nurses removing giant gauze pads soaked with blood from underneath her again and again until they had filled a garbage bag, but no doctor came.

My mind raced. After losing our baby, was I also going to lose my wife? Still, no doctor came. Standing in that hallway, I had never felt so alone.

In the midst of my anger and hopelessness, the lessons of my childhood surfaced again. For the first time in years, I closed my eyes and prayed, *"Jesus, please save my wife. Please save Sue."*

Minutes later, a nurse came out and said to me, "The bleeding has stopped. Your wife is lucky."

Was it the prayer or a coincidence? I didn't know and I didn't care. Sue was alive.

She was pale, her eyes were still closed and her eyebrows squeezed together. I lifted her hand. Her fingers felt cold and fragile. I rubbed them to bring back the warmth. "Sue? Can you hear me? I love you."

"I love you, too," she whispered, without opening her eyes. "I'm sorry about the baby." Her unexpected apology made me shut my eyes tightly.

An infection kept my wife in the hospital for seven days. During that week, I thought about the loss of the baby and Sue's brush with death and I blamed God for all that had happened to us.

In the following months as Sue recovered, I became even more angry and depressed. I lost my job and we were forced to sell our home and move in with my mother-in-law. God had truly forsaken me.

When Sue was well enough, we tried again to start a family. A year passed without success. We worried that she might not be able to conceive again and my anger and depression grew. Sue continued to pray for help, but I knew I was on my own.

Then, September 11, 2001, happened.

We did not know anyone lost in that terrible tragedy, yet we felt great sorrow. This time, when Sue suggested we go to church, I agreed. With heavy hearts, we prayed for the souls of those who had died.

Two weeks later, we moved into a place of our own and on the same day we were blessed with the discovery that we had a baby on the way. I had not prayed for either of these things. Could this be God's way of letting me know I was not alone after all?

Sue just smiled and we prayed together that the baby would be healthy. The first ultrasound was tense, but with Sue's help, I kept my faith. I believed everything would be fine.

We now have three healthy boys. My six-year-old son is constantly showing me his accomplishments and seeking my approval, which makes me proud. My four-year-old likes to sit on my lap when I am working on the computer or when we are watching his favorite movies. He snuggles in, calling it our "special time," and my heart swells with love.

Every time my 17-month-old son sees me, he screams, "Da Da!" and crawls toward me at high speed. He knows how to walk, but crawling is faster and safer when his brothers are around. I pick him up and hug him, eliciting big smiles from both of us.

Our boys have given new purpose and meaning to our lives, and prayer and meditation have become a regular part of our days. We have experienced their power and discovered that the act of praying for others brings miracles into your life and theirs.

I now know that helping others in any way brings happiness. I am ready to help on a greater and more active scale as a positive influence to the world.

The path I am on now is driven by a strong need to let others know that despite setbacks in life, even though they may be tragic, you must keep your faith. Sue and I are dedicated to personal growth and service because that is the only way we can ever feel truly fulfilled.

Nick DeCastro

IN SERVICE TO OUR CHILDREN: MOM AS EDUCATOR
Ellen M. Wilson, M.M.

C an a woman pursue her own career and homeschool her six-year-
old at the same time? Well, I'm about to find out. The decision to
homeschool my son might not seem so extraordinary in and of itself.
After all, I am a part-time faculty member at the local university.
Perhaps it is because I teach part-time, have very little experience teaching children, am releasing my debut CD and am being published in two
books that makes my choice to homeschool this year seem so dramatic.

However, my son asked me to do this. I want him to know I am there
for him in every way, so why should this be any different? I contemplat-
ed my options and thought about my choices. Why couldn't I homeschool? After all, I know a number of smart, educated women who have
set aside their own careers and ambitions in order to be a more intimate
molder and shaper of their children's educations.

Why couldn't I take all of my own education, experience and skills and
utilize them for the task of educating my son, especially as he enters his
primary school years? Why would educating other children be more
important than educating my own son? More importantly, perhaps,
what am I teaching my child if I say, "no," to him on this subject,
declining the opportunity to serve him in this greater way?

Certainly, for me, it would be a decidedly counter-cultural experience to
homeschool. Why, half of my family thought I had lost my mind when
they heard what I was considering. In addition, I wasn't willing to give
up my own ambitions and aspirations, being deeply immersed in a
number of important professional projects. Was there a way to homeschool as well?

Moreover, why would I go to all this trouble, to do all the extra work of
homeschooling when there are so many fine schooling choices? In the

end, I decided I would have to try. There was no other way to know for certain.

I became aware of the many resources around me, noting the examples set by others. The homeschooling mothers I know have indeed put their own education and resources to the service of educating their children. For example, there was a nurse who stopped practicing so she could devote herself full-time to the education of her four children, a primary-school teacher who changed her course when she realized she was dropping off her children at daycare in order to educate other people's children, and a former Army officer who tired of the constant separations and wanted her life to center around family, so she created a home-based business in order to stay home and homeschool her five children.

Once I thought of these women, I began to see the benefits of being my son's primary teacher. I realized how amazing it was that he actually asked me to teach him! His behavior toward his preschool teacher had been so much better than his behavior toward me that I was surprised he wanted me to teach him. When I asked him why, he replied simply, "So we can spend more time together." Suddenly, his request made sense. I had spent the majority of his life singing and teaching. Although I had shortened my work hours enormously for the first four years, I had spent the bulk of the last year involved in two CD projects. Those projects took much of my attention and required my presence away from home for the first time in his life.

I began to experience the wonderful challenge of learning with my son, the flexibility of being able to travel to places about which we had studied and to delve more fully into subjects that deeply interested him, as well as those that challenged him. The adventure of embarking upon this educational journey together was a chance for growth that I could enjoy as much as he would.

To be certain, in many ways I walk a solitary path. I don't know any other homeschooling mom from my cultural background with one child who has quite so many personal and professional ambitions, but most of us feel we walk a solitary path from time to time in our lives. Consider the examples I cited above. I am sure all of my friends have felt themselves to be walking a path of solitude at one time or another.

It actually feels great to walk an unblazed trail. Strangely enough, it has been through the process of decision-making that went against the tide of others that has helped me feel more confident about my decision.

As I talk to other friends about their own choices, my motto has become: find your voice. I do not mean as a singer, though that obviously holds true. I do not mean as a writer, though that also holds true. I mean as a human being, having the courage to walk your path, speaking up for what you know to be true and finding the voice that is yours alone. Join me in finding your own path—in service.

Ellen M. Wilson, M.M.

FAITHFUL SERVICE
Kevin Seney, B.S., M.B.A.

I began working with my father as a young boy and this early experience provided me with a life-long foundation of the value of serving others.

I was born and raised in a small town in Wyoming where our family owned the local drugstore. My great grandfather built the store in 1920 and my dad joined the business in 1958, the year I was born. There were many family-owned businesses back then, so it was the norm for kids to start working at an early age. I loved to work and I especially enjoyed working alongside my dad in the pharmacy.

Every evening, my dad and I would deliver prescriptions on our way home for dinner. I was his "runner." I knew by the way our customers welcomed me that the service we provided was very important to them. Wyoming winters are long and harsh, so my dad drove an old 4x4 Jeep to make sure we could always get across town with our deliveries. People knew they could depend on us. I learned at a very young age the importance of serving your community.

Our town was a ranch community, and we extended credit to the local families, knowing they would charge their purchases all year and pay us in the fall. Sometimes a harsh winter would hit, but my dad never worried about getting paid. He would just carry them until they got caught up. He never doubted people would pay. I remember a few times when some accounts got very big and the customers went for several years without paying. Then, one day, they would walk in and pay the entire balance in full. My father believed in trusting people.

We had several key employees who worked for our family for many years. They were all treated like extended family. They were invited to our home for Thanksgiving and other holiday parties. Years later, just before I headed off to college, I volunteered to drive one of our former employees to the VA hospital in the next town. He was terminally ill and could no longer care of himself. When I dropped him off at the hospital, he shook my hand with tears in his eyes, knowing he would not leave there alive. He had worked for our family for many years and I didn't realize until that moment we were the only family he had left. Sadly, he died a short time later, but I am glad I took the time to drive him.

Living my life in service to others came naturally to me as a result of modeling myself after my father. Values like honesty, integrity and service were a regular part of living and working in a small community. I did not realize then how much this experience would influence my career as an adult.

I was a natural salesman. Not because I was a "deal closer," but because I was a "relationship opener." My first career out of college was working as a loan officer for a fast-growing savings and loan firm. I moved up the ranks very quickly and was always willing to share my ideas and skills with my fellow loan officers. I was soon working directly with the CEO and executive vice president, developing strategies for sales training, marketing and recruiting.

I love the old Chinese proverb, "Give a man a fish and you feed him for a day. Teach a man to fish and you feed him for a lifetime." When your motives are based on "teaching people to fish" and providing a valuable service to others, the resulting business will thrive and grow.

The greatest lesson I have learned is that running a business is not just about making money, it is about serving people.

Kevin Seney, B.S., M.B.A.

OH, OLIVER! (FROM THE WAKE UP LIVE MOVIE)
Liz Vassey

I was a very, very, very shy kid when I was three or four. I just didn't talk to strangers and I was very uncomfortable in front of groups.

I started acting when I was nine, and I started in theater—actually musical theater. It was then that I saw my sister in a play, and I went to my mom, and I said, "I think I would really like to try that." She said, "Oh, I think that would be great. I'm not taking you. Your sister can take you out. I don't want any part of seeing you get up on that stage and seeing what happens."

The first play I auditioned for was *Oliver* and I sang for it, and I played Oliver. I remember getting up on that stage and actually feeling very much at home for the first time.

Once you've had that moment, I would say you have to be incredibly persistent. Do not believe too much of the good or of the bad. Stay true to yourself because they are trying to change you and fix you and mold you. I think what's different or peculiar about you is what's special about you in the first place. Don't lose it.

Liz Vassey

PAINTING FROM THE HEART
Gwen Fox

My life was busy with children, soccer games, tennis tournaments, track meets and home management. I painted when time permitted. I was conveniently busy, yet knew in an unconscious way that my busyness was an excuse to avoid looking within and asking myself what I wanted for *me*. Others thought my art was a hobby, but in my soul, I knew it was my life.

While I was growing up on a farm in eastern Tennessee, my mother wallpapered the hall of our old farmhouse and allowed me to draw on the walls. She re-papered each week for years. This is where I developed my creativity. I lived a childhood from which dreams are made.

After college, I married and soon realized not all people want the best for you. After 24 years of struggle, we divorced. Several years later, I remarried and began taking art workshops. They were good, but something was missing. I realized there was a mental component I needed and I started reading and discovering how the mind works. I also meditated—all in the hope of reaching a deeper level of self.

I soon discovered I had adopted those inner tapes of projected stories, lies and failures as my own, only to have their voices appear on my canvas. It was easy to believe the voices that said, "I can't" or "No one will like my art." They were comfortable and they had been with me all my life.

During this period, I was asked to teach art to adults. Insecure of my own place in the art world, I struggled with feelings of inferiority. I lacked an art degree, I was afraid of rejection and I was dyslexic. Despite all this, I agreed.

Because of what I needed for fulfillment in my teaching, I decided to include how the mind relates to creativity. Of my students, 99.9 percent were women and the mind-creativity connection resonated deeply with them. These were women who had raised families, some on their own. We had corporate leaders, entrepreneurs and stay-at-home moms—all out of their element. I observed them as they entered the classroom. Some were hoping against all hope they would be able to produce what was in their hearts, but past experiences told them they would be unsuccessful. Getting past this was a huge hurdle. When they approached their assignments, I could feel their fear. In order to get to the other side of creativity, they had to learn they had the right to paint and draw below their expectations. They were all afraid of failure.

We have all read the stories of people who have failed before reaching success, yet we don't equate this with ourselves. Stories of others experiencing the abyss of failure to get to eventual success are inspiring, but they only help if one allows that philosophy to become his own.

Without realizing it, most women present themselves in the way they think others want them to be. They start to paint to please others because it is painful to remove the social mask that has been with them for a lifetime. I know this because I wore one for many years. Over time, the door opens a bit and colorful possibilities present themselves, never to be forgotten. This is the magic of removing the layers that bind us to our preconceived ideas about ourselves. There is no longer the duality of "the artist and me." They become one. The most intriguing part is that it doesn't take much to remove these destructive, invasive thoughts. Providing a safe place and freedom for many glorious failures is uplifting and removes years of fear and defeat from our shoulders.

When women become comfortable with their innate passion, they will share it with others and the entire world will benefit. A confident mother is an excellent role model for her children—especially her daughters. They see her as eager and willing to go out and try new things without the fear of failure, because failure is an acceptable part of success.

My students learned to paint from the heart with conscious awareness. They are now able to hear their intuition and believe those distant thoughts. To watch their faces and see the confidence building is like witnessing a miracle. Their posture becomes different; the air surrounding them is one of anticipation. The fear is gone because they now view themselves as filled with purpose and fulfilling a desire and passion that has been stirring within them for many years. I realize this transformation occurs in many situations, but sometimes we forget how simple it is to help another enter that quiet space within their mind and to believe in their abilities for the first time.

When given the opportunity to let go of fear, the students discovered that facing their fears makes those fears smaller. They discovered they had more resources to call on and could now capture images they didn't know existed. They could believe in themselves as professional artists, not just as Sunday painters.

Facing their fears with painting also allowed these women to face other fears in their lives. One student quit her job, went back to school and now teaches art to children. Another worked through the loss of a child. Finding your passion gives you permission to look within and believe. We are all creative in some fashion, but we must remove our masks, which takes courage.

The women I have come to know and love are courageous, strong and bullheaded. I am proud of them because that is what it takes to crash through whatever holds you back. Serving and helping others to develop confidence, courage and belief in themselves has been a gift to me. It has filled my life with grace.

Gwen Fox

As Ye Give, So Shall Ye Receive
Vince Garvin

I am the fourth of eight children. I was born on a run-down council estate in London 50 years ago. My dad, a hopeless alcoholic, went out one day when I was 10 years old and I've never seen him since.

Things were different in those days because women had few rights. The rent book for the council house we lived in was in my father's name, which meant it was his house. Once he left, we were told we would have to get out.

I was placed in a foster home. My brothers and sisters were split up, given to other foster parents or put into care homes. My mother had no choice but to go back home and stay with her parents. She could have simply accepted that was the way it was, found another man and started over. In those days it would have been easier that way, but not my mum's way. She refused to let her family be split apart by the authorities. She took them to court and, against all the odds, she won. All nine of us were re-housed in a new council house. It only had three bedrooms and my mum had to sleep on the settee, but we couldn't believe our luck.

To keep us all together, my mum had to work day and night. She was up in the morning for her cleaning job, to the market to work through the day and to the local pub at lunchtimes and evenings to wait tables. In the afternoons, she came home to make dinner for us. Not once did I hear her complain.

What I didn't know was that she had made a vow. She had almost lost her children because we had been dependent on council care. She would never let anyone control her again and she was going to buy her own home.

She saved every spare penny. Every week, without exception, she would put something aside, no matter how small. It took her eight years to save the £3,000 she thought was enough for a deposit on a house.

She approached all the lending institutions. One after another, they turned her down. It was not considered safe to lend a single mother money to buy her own home. She had too many children and too little income.

Undeterred, she carried on. There was nothing she could do about being a woman or having eight children. She knew the only variable was her income. She had a flash of brilliance. Instead of buying a small house that she probably couldn't afford, she would buy a great big house that she definitely couldn't afford and rent out the spare rooms to lodgers. Presto! Extra income was on its way.

She found an eight-bedroom guest house in Margate, Kent. It was £11,750. Miraculously, this time she found a lender. When they refused to give her more than £5,000, she paid a deposit of £3,000 and borrowed the other £3,750 on an interest-only loan from the vendors themselves. Her drive, determination, persistence and belief had paid off. At 75, she is still buying old houses, renovating and selling them. Always laughing, always upbeat, always positive, she is an absolute inspiration to all who meet her.

Watching her over the years, I have learned that giving is the key to wealth. My mum had nothing after my dad disappeared but his debts and eight kids to look after, but she has dedicated her entire life to the well-being of all of us. She has taken nothing for herself. She has given her entire life to her children. All of us are now family people, in good relationships and home owners who are happy and well-balanced. Some of us are pretty successful financially, too. This, my mum says, is her reward. She has lived and worked hard to see all of us together, happy, healthy and wealthy.

Following in the shadow of my mum, I put into practice the lessons learned from watching her for all of those years. I started a company dedicated to helping others reach their goals and targets and to realize their ambitions and aspirations. We have provided sales training, inspiration and the motivation to succeed. I have worked with literally thousands of people. I listen, spend time with them and show them that with passion, drive and determination, they can achieve almost anything. I show them that working for the good of others is a much greater motivation than any personal goal. In 1994, I employed three people. By 1999, I employed 350, all dedicated to helping others improve the quality of their lives. Please try to understand there is a distinct difference between "standard of living" and "quality of life."

Money can bring a high standard of living, whereas working for the good of others, giving your time and experience and nurturing good, healthy relationships will bring you immense satisfaction and, therefore, a great quality of life. I sold that company in 2000 and now help people start, expand and improve their own businesses. Dedicated to serving others, we have been successful once more.

I have an observation. I have traveled the world, seen its most affluent places and its poorest. I have met rich businessmen and people with more wealth than they know what to do with, but they so often seem frustrated and angry. Dissatisfied, they have affairs and their marriages don't last. They always seem to want more. They have fallen into the habit of taking from the world. In the poorest areas of the world I have seen the most amazing acts of generosity. It's ironic, but the people who have the least are often the ones who are most willing to give, and often they're much happier for it.

If you really want to make a difference in your own life, dedicate yourself to making a difference in the lives of others. The more you help other people get what they want, the more other people will help you get what you want. Please try to understand this concept, as it really does work. And remember, as ye give, so shall ye receive. May all your dreams come true.

Vince Garvin

THE JOY OF SERVICE
Warren Broad, C.C.H.T., M.F.T.

Did you know service is actually something that benefits *you* more than others? This may come as a surprise to you, but as an addiction counselor and a firefighter, every occasion I have had to assist others in either field has rewarded me with immense joy. The source of this joy is the ability to apply the wisdom I've gained over the years in a meaningful, worthwhile way to help others.

I once had an addiction client who still stands out in my mind. "John" had been drinking for 30 years and came to me in a very depressed state. I saw in him a man with a troubled past who needed someone to be there for him. As I listened to his life story, I assured him that, although I was younger than he, I deeply understood his desire for change.

Over the next several months, I worked with John on understanding his inner addiction, including the desires and nature of the addictive mind. I taught him to not give into his temptations and I provided some tests for him to complete in order to identify the true nature of his addiction. John soon realized the addiction was something separate from his interior self. He did not have to obey it and it could, in fact, be controlled. He then established a target date for total sobriety. I assured him he was not alone—someone was always there for him. This allows clients to feel the confidence they need to succeed. John has now been sober for a year and his health has dramatically improved.

I eventually moved from Toronto to Muskoka, Canada, and wanted to become active in my new community. A gentleman I ran into suggested volunteer firefighting. I had always respected firemen, so I opted to try his recommendation. After some training and tests, I was officially part of the crew.

As a firefighter, I have had the pleasure of making a difference when it's truly needed on an immediate basis. A volunteer does dangerous work and endures some very disturbing situations with very little monetary compensation. However, it is the deeply consoling reward that comes from a pure desire to help others that I find most satisfying. We are also able to see the benefits of our work immediately.

I have seen my firefighting work make a difference on several occasions. Once, my department was called to rescue a woman who had slipped and fallen into a dangerous set of rapids in a provincial park. As a certified lifeguard, I felt my skills would be helpful. She had broken her leg and it was twisted between two rocks. The level of teamwork required in order to get her to safety was inspiring. I can still recall the adrenaline that was coursing through my veins as I stepped into my car soaking wet and left the scene after the rescue. I am still amazed at how blessed I am to have discovered that serving others is what truly brings me joy.

As the child of an alcoholic and witness to other friends and family who dealt with their addictions in different ways, I decided to study addictions and human behavior. I watched my mother struggle and it was difficult to endure. However, I used this knowledge to learn a safe pattern of behavior for myself. When a friend of mine started down the road of cocaine addiction, I immediately did a large amount of research on the subject, as well as on other drugs. This would be beneficial for me in the future when, as a counselor, I would have to assess the level of addiction in others.

Following the death of my mother, I fell into a deep depression that lasted many months. However, I was led though this difficulty to find my purpose in life, which is helping others with similar problems. I found work as a counselor for teens in a group home. Many of the residents had similar experiences growing up. I decided to take courses in adult psychology, which I followed up with a course in counseling. I left the group home and started a private practice where I specialized in clinical hypnosis and focused on addictions and compulsions.

My purpose in life is service and I am dedicated to saving as many lives in as many ways as I can. I am blessed to have survived the challenges in my life, and my goal is to be the best counselor possible. As addictions and compulsive behaviors become more prevalent, I will continue to provide my clients with an environment in which I can be there for them unconditionally.

Serving others is as much a gift to me as it is for those I help.

Warren Broad, C.C.H.T., M.F.T.

DON'T YOU JUST LOVE IT!
Lee Beard

Don't you just love it when you get good service, especially when you don't have to ask for it? It's even better when it's service with a smile. The day seems to get brighter and it encourages you to give that smile away to others. Unfortunately, this kind of service is far too rare in our fast-paced world. I especially notice it when I am traveling and dining, but for the most part, retail stores and attitudes have gone to "self serve."

I would like to say that I do a good job at encouraging others to give me good service. However, many times I find my mind is on the mission for the moment, so I fail to think of the other person and give him or her a smile. We are instructed to "love God with all of our heart, soul, mind and strength" and "love our neighbor as our self." It's a good thing that we do not have to do this in our own strength but can rely on God to love through us. Otherwise, I would be in big trouble.

What motivates us to serve? We have a saying in the marketing world that our customers are tuned to the radio station WIIFM: "What's In It For Me?" In order to give good service, we need to be aware of what our friends, family and customers want or need. Then, we need to take the time to approach them from their point of view. It doesn't sound too difficult, but it does take time and thoughtfulness. This is something that we are not always willing to give.

If there is one thing I know that helps in our personal, social and professional lives, it is the ability to be kind. People will welcome you in most any situation if they know that you are a nice person. Recently, we talked with some television executives and they mentioned that they preferred to work with nice people. I don't know anyone who would not appreciate doing business with someone who is nice.

Don't you just love it when people are nice and treat you kindly? You can have lots of people who want to do business with you when you make it a habit to give good service and to be exceptionally nice. It's just good business!

Enjoy!

Lee Beard

Author Index

Born in New York, Nury spent the first six years of her life in the city. After graduating from school, she worked and traveled to find herself. Through her research she found hypnosis. She always knew the mind was a powerful tool, so she became a clinical hypnotherapist and counselor, opening Circle of Harmony. She is now working for people through seminars, groups, schools and individuals throughout New Jersey.

Telephone: Office 973-424-1469 or Cell 201-970-6309
Web site: www.circleofharmony.org
E-mail: circleharmony8@aol.com

Shabana was introduced to a book and a concept that forever changed her life. The information she received taught her how to change results by changing the way she thought. Today Shabana travels as a public speaker, life coach and teaches thousands of people how to develop and utilize the skills that changed her life. Many people achieve financial success, but Shabana teaches people how to achieve true life success.

Address: Calgary, Alberta, Canada
Telephone: 1-800-565-1268, 403-616-6091
Web site: www.IntegrityHumanCapital.com
E-mail: LifeSuccess@shaw.ca

As a certified BodyTalk™ practitioner, Jessica loves to help women achieve their optimal health and inner peace. Her passion is uniting people around the globe through the universal language of the body. She is an author, speaker, health coach and founder of the non-profit organization Inner Peace IS World Peace, Inc. For extra info and bonuses or to connect with Jessica please call or visit her online at www.JessicaArdeal.com.

Inner Peace IS World Peace. Dream it. Feel it. Know it. Live it.
Inner Peace IS World Peace, Inc.
Telephone: 1-877-75-PEACE
Web site: www.innerpeaceISworldpeace.org

Author and CEO, OneCoach.
The Answer: Grow Any Business, Achieve Financial Freedom, and Live an Extraordinary Life
Telephone: 858-792-1250
Web site www.ReadTheAnswer.com
E-mail: Info@OneCoach.com

Bacon, Brett E., Esq. 115
Brett E. Bacon, Esq., is founder and CEO of MyLife Franchise Corporation, a national, retail, hearing healthcare franchise company. He is a self-made millionaire, attorney-at-law, retired U.S. Army Judge Advocate General Officer, author, business coach and speaker. He is the author of *Millionaire Selling Secrets*, (2009©).

To learn more about his other books and services, go to www.brettbacon.com
Telephone: Toll free 866-480-1220
E-mail: info@brettbacon.com

Beard, Lee 199
Lee is a television producer, advertising executive and business developer. He lives in Arkansas when not traveling as the co-creator of the *Wake Up...Live the Life You Love* book series. Lee is an author featured in more than a dozen motivational and inspirational volumes. He concentrates on bringing the power of the Wake Up network to bear on the challenges of business development. If you've had a "wake up" moment you would like to share, visit wakeupmoment.com to tell your story!

Web site: www.wakeupmoment.com, www.wakeuplive.net, leebeard.com
E-mail: lee@wakeuplive.net

Beckwith, Dr. Michael 77
Founder and Spiritual Director.

Agape International Spiritual Center
Address: Culver City, CA
Web site: www.agapelive.com

Belton, Aine 153
Aine Belton is the founder of Miracle Mind, the Global Love Project and Divine Gateways. She has coached thousands of people through her books, courses and programs which include the Miracle Mind Manifesting Program, Belief Buster Kit and Divine Mentoring Program.

Web sites: www.miracle-mind.com, www.globalloveproject.com, www.divinegateways.com
E-mail: aine@miracle-mind.com

Bourke, Tony 171
Tony Bourke is a director of AIIB Pty. Ltd., providing insurance advice and associated services to business owners. Tony has another book being released in 2009 called *Risk Your Business, Risk Your Life*. The book will provide business owners with insurance tips, information and secrets that will help them to protect their business. Tony lives with his wife and family on the Central Coast of NSW, Australia.

Author, Speaker, Adviser, Director
Web sites: www.tonybourke.com.au, www.aiib.com.au

Dr. Bowman received her medical degree from Wake Forest University School of Medicine and her "Mrs." in 1977. She completed pediatric training in 1980 at Baylor College of Medicine in Houston, Texas. She has learned, and continues to learn, from her four wonderful children and many wonderful families in her hometown of North Wilkesboro, North Carolina. She is working on her health coaching certification, helping others be their best!

Special Care for Special Kids & Adult Preventive Health, Inc.
Address: 702 Thirteenth St., P.O. Box 128
N. Wilkesboro, NC 28659
Telephone: 336-667-6444 Fax: 336-667-4515

Warren Broad lives in Huntsville, Canada where he practices and lives with his wife, son and two dogs. Visit Npch.ca to contact Warren at any time.

Clinical Hypnotherapist
Marriage, Family and Individual Therapist
Volunteer Firefighter
Web site: www.npch.ca
E-mail: info@npch.ca

Dr. Liliana Cerepnalkoski is a medical intuitive, energy healer and lecturer. She is a pioneer and a new voice in the fields of medical intuition, energy medicine, human consciousness and transformation. A gifted clairvoyant and a physician-scientist with a diverse background of study in general medicine, cancer research, AIDS research, intuition, spirituality and metaphysics, Liliana bridges the realms of Science and Spirit. Available for office and phone consultations.

Address: 1010 N. Central Ave.
Glendale, CA 91202
Telephone: 310-772-8270 Fax: same
Web Site: www.DrLiliana.com
E-Mail: info@DrLiliana.com

The Inspired Entrepreneur's Network is a group of independent business owners in the field of personal development. They work in collaboration with the power of leveraging and collective thinking to create greater levels of financial success. This win-win model benefits both individual business owners and the larger community. As self-conscious entrepreneurs, they will grow personally and become financially empowered while helping others do the same. To learn more visit the Web site below.

Conscious Entrepreneurs Network (Part of the Freedom Community)
Web site: www.LeadershipAndAbundance.com

Johanna is a writer, teacher, Licensed Professional Counselor and Certified Confidence Coach in private practice in Portland, OR. She is also an ordained minister through the Association for the Integration of the Whole Person. Her work seeks to help people heal from the mis-truths they've been taught, and to build a core of self-love, awareness, empowerment, ease and integrity—internally and in their relationships with others. She is available for in-person and telephone counseling and coaching consultations, as well as for workshops and speaking engagements.

Web site: www.jcourtleigh.com

E-mail: johanna@jcourtleigh.com

    Love is what life is all about—fun, health, happiness, true wealth and success all depend on love. Dr. Anne Curtis is a successful sexual and relationship therapist, physician, energy healer and self-help consultant. She teaches what love is really all about and how you can enjoy every aspect of your life to the fullest through loving relationships.

Web sites: www.makeloveforlife.com, www.succeed4sure.com, www.quantumhealingHQ.com, www.winwinoffer.com

E-mail: love@makeloveforlife.com

    Nick DeCastro is a success coach who "woke up" one day and realized his true calling was to serve others by helping them achieve their goals and turn dreams into reality. Nick's humor and unique approach to coaching make clients choose Nick as their accountability partner. He is also a sought-after speaker, trainer and author. He currently lives in Toronto with his wife and three sons.

Telephone: 416-253-4745

Web site: www.nickdecastro.com

E-mail: iam@nickdecastro.com

    Mara is a motivational speaker and a Certified Dream Coach. She helps people get clear on what is really important to them, and then, with a remarkable program and process that was taught to her by Marcia Wieder of Dream Coach University, she helps people make their dreams come true.

Certified Dream Coach

For a one-hour complimentary coaching consultation, please call:

Telephone: 407-909-9570

E-mail: Maradiamond@msn.com

Alison has committed herself to helping others expand their knowledge and inner desires through her Web site. She offers downloadable information regarding self-development, relationships, business, real estate, finance and health. She calls Brisbane, Australia her home.

Director, (BBusMan, DipEd)
OneStop Success International Pty Ltd
Telephone: +61 404 473 143
Web site: www.onestopsuccessclub.com
E-mail: alison@onestopsuccessclub.com

Best-selling author and lecturer.
Wayne is the author of these best-selling books: *Power of Intention, Real Magic, Manifesting Your Destiny* and *Pulling Your Own Strings.*

Susan obtained her bachelor's degree in biology from Wheaton College, Norton, MA and her master's degree in biology from the University of Virginia, Charlottesville, VA. As a gardener and earth-lover, she believes heaven is not just above our heads, but under our feet, as well.

Telephone: 757-291-1379 (mobile)
Web site: www.beachbutterflies.org

Gwen Fox is an internationally known artist, teacher and speaker. Her work is in museums, publications and private collections. As a coach and mentor, Gwen empowers others to find their creative genius. She teaches throughout the United States. Gwen shares the mind-creativity connection in each workshop.

Telephone: 719-440-3874
Web site: www.gwenfox.com
E-mail: gwen@gwenfox.com

At age 12, Vince was building push-bikes and selling them at auction. At 15, he trained as a carpenter and joiner. Thirty years later, Vince has started, built, successfully ran and sold several businesses. He is a true entrepreneur; the thrill of a new business venture is still central to his dynamic ethos. A family man, sports enthusiast and larger-than-life character, Vince's experience and personality will inspire you to take on the world, and win!

Web site: www.vincegarvin.co.uk
E-mail: vince@vincegarvin.co.uk

Ruben Gonzalez has competed in three Olympics in three separate decades. He is an award-winning keynote speaker and the best-selling author of *The Courage to Succeed*, and the co-star of *Pass It On*. Ruben gives over 90 presentations a year on the subject of making bold decisions and taking action to create long-lasting success. To watch Ruben's 33-minute video filled with success tips, get his free 10-Part Success eCourse or to check Ruben's availability to speak at your next event, please call or go to his Web site.

Telephone: 832-689-8282
Web site: www.TheOlympicSpeaker.com

A best-selling co-author, David Goodall has become known for his motivational speeches that have helped people from all walks of life. His debt-reduction techniques have allowed many people to gain control of their finances and prosper. The name of his company, DieselDog, signifies the internal diesel engine and the loyalty of the dog. You need to be loyal and focused on your dreams and visions to make them a reality.

Web sites: www.DieselDogEnterprises.com, www.grabmywheel.com
E-mail:dave@dieseldogenterprises.com

A sought-after speaker, author and workshop leader, Bill Harris is founder and director of Centerpointe Research Institute and creator of Holosync® audio technology. Started in 1989 with borrowed recording equipment set up on his kitchen table, Centerpointe now has over 150,000 Holosync® users in 172 countries.

Centerpointe Research Institute
Address: 1700 NW 167th Pl., Suite 220
Beaverton, OR 97006
Telephone: 800-945-2741
Web site: www.centerpointe.com

Ernie is currently acting and writing for TV and film and is available for speaking and personal appearances. Ernie has performed in various TV shows, movies and plays, including *Taxi, OZ, Ghost Busters, The Hand that Rocks the Cradle, Congo, Miss Congeniality, The Crow* and a variety of others. He has also written two published plays, *Rebellion 369* and *My Kingdom Come*, and is working on others in the near future. His personal representative, Thomas Cushing, can be contacted at Innovative Artist, 310-656-0400, and Ernie can be reached through his Web site.

Web site: www.Ernie-Hudson.com.

Jones, Andrew *91*
    Andrew Jones was born in London in 1968 and eventually left school with no qualifications. Although he worked his way up the corporate ladder in London for 23 years and earned a place in management, he was stuck in a place he never belonged until July 2007, when he realized his dream by completing his first book and CD, *Awakenings*.

Managing Director InfoMarkit Limited
Address: Tunbridge Wells, Kent United Kingdom
Telephone: +44 1892 614445 (work), +44 17854 907677 (mobile)
E-mail: andrew@infomarkit1.com

Lee, Vickie *15*
    Vickie Lee combines her natural intuitive abilities with a variety of healing modalities to bring better energy for better health. Vickie provides a beautiful, safe, relaxing environment for you to enjoy her nurturing treatments that will transform how you look, feel and experience life.

Aqua Lea
Telephone: 916-984-6606
Web site: www.aqualeahealth.com
E-mail: vickieb@sbcglobal.net

Lestz, Jeffrey *3*
    Jeffrey Lestz is co-CEO of Genistar, Limited, a London based financial education and services firm with 14 offices throughout the UK. Jeff has over 30 years of experience in business and has coached thousands of people to financial independence and business ownership. He has taught seminars throughout Europe and the U.S. Jeff and his wife, Margo, live between London, England and Nice, France.

Co-CEO, Genistar, Ltd.
Address: 27 Old Gloucester Street BM Box 5310
London, UK WC1N 3XX
Web site: www.Genistar.net
E-mail: jeff.lestz@genistar.net

Levi, Zachary *49*
    At the early age of six, Zachary began acting, singing and dancing in school and local theater productions. He has performed in regional roles such as *Grease, The Outsiders, Oliver, The Wizard of Oz* and *Big River*. But, it was his portrayal of Jesus in Ojai's *Godspell* that brought him to the attention of Hollywood. He completed a supporting role in the television movie *Big Shot: Confessions of a Campus Bookie* (2002) (TV). He then began acting as Kipp Steadman in the TV series *Less Than Perfect* (2002) and was also seen in the television movie *See Jane Date* (2003) (TV) on the WB. He also stars in NBC's *Chuck*. In his spare time, Zachary enjoys skateboarding, snowboarding, skydiving and participating in various other sports (Bio information obtained from www.IMDB.com).

As a teacher/learner and school administrator, Joe Lone has great faith in life education. Being actively engaged in each teachable moment has kept him intrigued because of the gifts we share. Semi-retirement has opened the door to the great school of life and marvelously magnified the awareness and rewards.

> Address: PH6 - 100 County Court Blvd
> Brampton, ON L6W 3X1
> E-mail: josephlone@gmail.com

Steve Mass, president of National Credit League (NATCRL), began his journey of improving people's financial lives in 2004. Partnering with 7 Steps to 720© credit education program, Steve launched the seminar and coaching program in Southern California. Since then, the 7 Steps to 720© program has been expanded throughout the U.S. A few years later, not completely satisfied, Steve created an even better way of improving people's financial lives and founded NATCRL in 2008 to expand his vision of educating Americans on the rules of credit.

> Web site: www.nationalcreditleague.com
> E-mail: commissioner@natcrl.com

Formally educated and trained as a pharmacist, Frank had his "Wake Up" moment after rediscovering his spirituality and creative spark. His art is a reflection of the personal duality between science and intuitive spiritual connection to the world. His art is informed by his extensive travels, including backpacking in Costa Rica, and spending time in Vietnam, Thailand, Laos, Hong Kong and Hawaii. Frank is passionate about his art and his spiritual journey and sharing these with the world.

> Frank Michael Art and Design
> Web sites: www.Frankmichael-Art-Design.com, www.MystikEgg.com
> E-mail: frank@frankmichael-art-design.com

Cheryl is an entrepreneur and community volunteer.

> Telephone: 425-503-9959
> Web site: www.thecolorcoachbellevue.com
> E-mail: colorcoach@gmail.com

Dr. Michael Mountain is a chiropractic neurologist treating lower back disc injuries with cutting edge technology. He provides behavior-reconditioning programs to those suffering with weight problems and chronic pain. He lives in San Diego with his wife and two children and also enjoys hiking, exercise, martial arts, neurology and brain research.

Southern California Spine Center—lower back and sciatica specialty center
Mindset for Health—behavior reconditioning tools for chronic pain and weight loss
Address: 7801 Mission Center Court, Suite 202
San Diego, CA 92108
Telephone: 619-692-0712
Web sites: www.southerncaliforniaspinecenter.com, www.mindsetforhealth.com

Margaret Fenton Munro arrived in Australia in 1974 at the age of 47 with her seven year-old son and $1. Over the last 30 years, she has experienced plenty of ups and downs, but love and gratitude have triumphed. The only way is up.

Address: P.O. Box 169 Mapleton
Qld 4560, Australia
Telephone: +617 54457343
Web site: www.margaretmunro.com
E-mail: healthy@margaretmunro.com

Dr. Michelle Nielsen is a chiropractor, entrepreneur and speaker. In her new book, *Manifesting Matisse: A Practical System for Reality Creation*, she shares a user-friendly, proven process that we can use to realize our visions for our lives and the world. Visit ManifestingMatisse.com today to join the MM Community and discover the action-based program people across the globe are calling "the user's manual" of *The Secret.*

Address: C/Pelai 11, 4E
Barcelona, 08001 Spain
Telephone: Int'l + 34+ 93-317-0066
Web sites: www.manifestingmatisse.com, www.mastermanifestor.com
E-mail: manifestingmatisse@gmail.com

João Dias de Oliveira was born in Patos de Minas, Minas Gerais, Brazil and has lived in Miami, Florida since 1981. He has worked for the United States Postal Service since 1987. His daughter, Cynthia Pino, was born in Miami and lives there with her husband, Jay, and her son, Christopher. Cynthia has published some of her poems. She's currently co-authoring two novels and editing three others.

Address: P.O.Box 14-4444
Coral Gables, FL 33114-4444
Telephone: 305-431-4786, 786-315-8362
E-mail: Jodiol@Yahoo.com, Cynthia.Pino@Yahoo.com

Judith has attracted everything she has in her life with this little secret. She loves what she does and does what she loves. Her job as a loan officer gives her the ability to help others and share the knowledge of positive thinking to help them get into the home of their dreams. She now has the home of her dreams, on the river with the outdoors and wildlife she enjoys.

E-mail: Judyspencer9518@yahoo.com

Creator of *Wake Up...Live the Life You Love*. With more than 12 million stories in print, his message is inspiring an international audience. Steven E has been joined in the book series by such noted speakers as Brian Tracy, John Assaraf and many more inspirational souls. He is now coaching select individuals on the development of a multimillion-dollar information business with their own message to inspire people around the world.

Web sites: stevene.com, wakeupstore.com/pcc

Vicki Jo is an educator with more than 12 years experience in religious education and event management. She holds a master's degree in communication and a specialist's degree in college teaching. Vicki Jo is the director of the Wake Up Live Foundation and has led medical mission teams to Sierra Leone.

Address: P.O. Box 894
Murray, KY 42071
Telephone: 270-753-5225
Web site: www.wakeuplivefoundation.org
E-mail: foundation@wakeuplive.net

Dr. Richard Tapper is a graduate of Southern California University of Health Sciences and is owner of two chiropractic clinics: Tapper Chiropractic and Family Chiropractic of Niverville. Dr. Tapper co-authored the highly successful book, *Tired of Being Sick and Tired.* He is an international speaker and his mission is to educate, adjust and inspire families toward wellness.

Address: Unit 1-1325 Markham Rd
Winnipeg, Manitoba, R3T 4J6
Telephone: 204-275-5030
E-mail: doctapper@hotmail.com

Brian Tracy is the most listened to audio author on personal and business success in the world today. His fast-moving talks and seminars on leadership, sales, managerial effectiveness and business strategy are loaded with powerful, proven ideas and strategies that people can immediately apply to get better results in every area.

Brian Tracy International
Address: 462 Stevens Ave., Suite 202
Solana Beach, CA 92075
Telephone: 858-436-7300
Web site: www.BrianTracy.com
E-mail: BrianTracy@briantracy.com

Born in Northern California, Robert has experienced many failures and successes in his life and has learned to overcome the obstacles put in front of him. He currently runs a successful consulting company. He helps people reach beyond their comfort zone so they too can achieve the things they desire.

Entrepreneur/Lifestyle Coach
Helping you achieve your dreams.
Web sites: robertbvance.com/blog/
E-mail: robertvance@robertbvance.com

She began acting at the age of nine (portraying Oliver in the musical of the same name) and continued to work extensively on the stage, performing in over 50 plays at regional and professional theaters in the Tampa Bay area. Liz has appeared as a regular or recurring character on nine television shows including *CSI, The Tick, Maximum Bob, Brotherly Love* and *All My Children* (for which she was nominated for a Daytime Emmy). Her hobbies are writing (she has sold two potential pilot scripts to studios), scuba diving and running (Bio information obtained from www.IMBD.com).

Becky West is an "Entrepreneur in Training," learning everything she needs to learn to deliver her message the best way she can. She is excited and confident that this is the first step to connect with you, the reader, to offer observation, insight and wisdom gained as a determined and persistent "student in action" of experts in the continuous learning industry.

Address: 207 2925 Qu'Appelle Street
Victoria, BC V9A 1V3
Telephone: 250-360-1188
Web site: www.iLearningGlobal.biz/download
E-mail: ilgcoach@gmx.com

Kandi White is a devoted wife and mother of two children. She is very thankful for the rich blessings God has bestowed on her life and is dedicated to helping others by sharing her gifts and talents. She wrote and self-published her first publication, *Hours of Pure Gold*, and she hopes that the motivational stories will inspire others to reach for their goals and dreams.

Address: KAW Enterprises
P.O. Box HM 1818
Hamilton, HM HX, Bermuda

An active performer and recording artist, Ellen is on the music faculty of the University of Texas at El Paso. Ellen's new CD, Songs of Ascent is receiving overwhelming praise for its uplifting spirituality and gorgeous ambience. As a teacher, performer and writer, Ellen endeavors to help others find their own voice in all matters. She is also a homeschooling mom.

Telephone: 915-449-3834
Web site: www.ellenmwilson.com
E-mail: Info@ellenmwilson.com

M. Rose Windels is an art teacher, television and script writer, director and producer and a public relations agent. She has also owned Roses Music Publishing CIE, a record business, for 25 years. For 12 years, she has been a profession رلكم birther, author, wellness coach and international lecturer. Her books include *Why Die if You Can Live* and *The Ultimate Truth Behind the Secret.* *"What if I were God…and you, und sie, et toi,   e voi!"*

Telephone: +3223462263 Mobile: +32497482550
Web site: www.abreathewithrose.vpweb.com
E-mail: abreathewithrose@skynet.be

RESOURCES

Centerpointe Research Institute
1700 NW 167th Place, Suite 220
Beaverton, OR 97006
800-945-2741

Centerpointe Research Institute offers two programs, The Holosync Solution and The Life Principles Integration Process. The Holosync Solution uses Centerpointe's proprietary Holosync audio technology to place the listener in states of deep meditation, creating dramatic and rapid changes in mental, emotional and spiritual health. Over 150,000 people in 172 countries have used Holosync to improve their lives. By filling out a short survey at www.centerpointe.com you can get a free Holosync demo CD and a special report about Holosync and how it works, or call 800-945-2741.

In Centerpointe's Life Principles Integration Process, you'll learn the internal processes you use to unconsciously and automatically create your internal and external results, and how to take control of this process so you can consciously and intentionally create the internal and external results you really want. For more information about The Life Principles Integration Process, and to hear a free preview lesson, visit www.centerpointe/preview.

RESOURCES

Early To Rise
866-344-7200
www.EarlyToRise.com

Early To Rise is the Internet's most popular health, wealth and success e-zine. Their purpose is to support their readers in a quest to succeed in life. When you sign up for Early To Rise, you will receive a message in your e-mail inbox every morning, full of good cheer and useful advice; you will be armed with loads of experience, useful insights and great resources.

Early To Rise wants you to succeed in any area of life you wish. They can give you inspiration or show you how it's done. Their goal is to get you to understand something, remember something, realize something and, ultimately, to do something that will make you healthier, wealthier and even wiser every day of the year.

When you read Early To Rise, you will be reminded of all that is possible for you. A better, brighter, fuller, and happier future is at your fingertips. Go to www.EarlyToRise.com to sign up for this free e-zine!

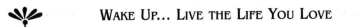

RESOURCES

Brian Tracy International
462 Stevens Ave Suite 202
Solana Beach, CA 92075
858-481-2977

Brian Tracy International offers three services: Brian Tracy Online, Brian Tracy University and Brian Tracy Speaking. Brian Tracy Online provides learning programs and educational materials to ensure success in the subjects of entrepreneurship, finance, management, personal development, sales, and time management. You will find an array of programs in CD, DVD and book format to assist in the development of your personal greatness. Visit the Web site at www.BrianTracy.com or call the customer service representatives at 858-481-2977. They are happy to discuss your personal needs and areas of focus to ensure the perfect learning program is selected.

Brian Tracy University is the perfect choice for students who are ambitious, persistent, self-reliant, disciplined, responsible, focused, committed to continuous learning and growth, as well as determined to increase their income and profits. Once you enroll in Brian Tracy University, Brian will teach you how to increase your sales and income, improve your revenues, cash flow and profits as well as how to become an excellent manager and leader, while boosting your personal productivity and performance. Brian has successfully helped thousands of people reach their personal and financial goals. Allow Brian Tracy to help you achieve these same goals by enrolling today! To speak with the National Enrollment Director, please call 858-481-2977.

Brian Tracy Speaking offers fast-moving, informative, enjoyable and entertaining presentations. Brian has a wonderful ability to customize each talk for his particular audience. He presents a series of great ideas and strategies with a rare combination of fact, humor, insights and practical concepts that audience members can apply immediately to get better results. To book a speaking event, please call Victor Risling at 858-481-2977.

WAKE UP...
LIVE THE LIFE YOU LOVE

In Service

NOETIC PYRAMID

Noetic Pyramid

The Noetic (no-EH-tik) Pyramid is a systemic way of looking at the benefits of learning and implementing the attitudes, beliefs and behaviors that must always precede real abundance in life.

NOESIS (no-ë´-sis, noun) [Greek. To perceive] 1. Philosophical: Purely intellectual apprehension. 2. Psychological: Cognition, especially through direct and self-evident knowledge. Noetic (adjective)

There is a way to know; therefore, there is a way to know what to do in life. The answers are not concealed from us, but are available through noesis: a purely intellectual process which gives us sure answers, if only we will look and grasp what we see.

But no one can see—or even look with energy and purpose—unless the mind is clear and the attention is directed. We need a guiding principle that gives us a direction and a foundation.

Building on what they have discovered over years of working with teachers, mentors, motivators, philosophers, psychologists and business leaders, Steven E and Lee Beard have devised the Noetic Pyramid: a structure of beliefs and learning that takes us from the firmest of foundations to the kind of life we can most enjoy; the kind of life which can most benefit those around us; the kind of life that may change the world.

Foundations
With your firm faith in God, you have the proper perspective to process all instructions that you receive. Then, when you give adequate attention to your health, you have a solid foundation to allow you to learn and utilize what we call "The 7 Secrets of Living the Life You Love."

Charting the Course
Then we must develop the internal structures of abundance: find your purpose through meditation or prayer, then visualize your desired future. To embark on this process without a firm grounding in belief and without the physical tools to support your mind and spirit, you are almost sure to be disappointed.

Reach Out to Expand the Possibilities
The Pyramid then leads you from a firm foundation to the external techniques of planning, teamwork, marketing and acquiring the necessary money. None of these external elements will be meaningful without the foundational elements, but neither will these essential elements inherently lead to abundance.

Abundance and Gratitude
We must realize the benefits of learning and utilize the internal structure and external techniques to create abundance, freedom, gratitude and fulfillment so we can truly live the life we love. An abundant life has meaning beyond ourselves, so we must seek to improve the lives of others. When we use our freedom to the benefit of others, when we are thankful for the opportunity to share the blessings of a materially abundant life, then we are fulfilled beyond our ability to imagine.

This is what we want everyone around the world to do: *Wake Up...Live the Life You Love.*

Wake Up...
Live the Life You Love

In Service

A Gift For You

Wake Up...Live the Life You Love wants to give you a gift that will get you moving on the path to personal abundance. Please visit www.wakeupgift.com today!